THE ⚜ TIMES

HOW TO PASS
GRADUATE
PSYCHOMETRIC
TESTS

2ND EDITION

Mike Bryon

**KOGAN
PAGE**

First published as *Graduate Recruitment Tests* in 1994
Reprinted in 1994 as *How to Pass Graduate Recruitment Tests*
Reprinted with revisions in 1995
Reprinted 1996, 1997, 1998
Second edition as *How to Pass Graduate Psychometric Tests* in 2001
Reprinted in 2002 (twice), 2003

Kogan Page Limited
120 Pentonville Road
London
N1 9JN

www.kogan-page.co.uk

© Mike Bryon, 1994, 2001

British Library Cataloguing in Publication Data

A CIP record for this book is available from the British Library.

ISBN 0 7494 3496 1

Typeset by Jean Cussons Typesetting, Diss, Norfolk
Printed and bound in Great Britain by Clays Ltd, St Ives plc

Contents

Preface iv

1. Psychometric tests 1

2. The maximum benefits of practice 7

3. Great candidate – except for the maths 15
   Part 1   A diagnostic exercise 17
   Part 2   Glossary 26
   Part 3   Practice questions 43
   Part 4   Mock tests 57

4 Relearn the rules of English usage 82
   Part 1   Glossary 83
   Part 2   Practice questions 96
   Part 3   Mock test 121

5. Lots more really relevant practice 133

6. Four mock tests to develop a winning test strategy 183

Preface

This book provides advice and practice exercises relevant to many of the tests used by employers to recruit managers and graduates. The practice exercises and mock tests are intended to allow the reader to build up speed, accuracy and confidence. Both a maths and a grammar glossary are provided to enable you to revise the rules of arithmetic and English usage. Advice is provided on the type and amount of practice you should undertake. Answers are provided at the end of each chapter. Doing well in a test is not simply down to intelligence but also requires you to be sufficiently motivated to want to pass and to try hard. In some cases, practice and a determination to do well will mean the difference between pass and fail.

This new edition is greatly enlarged and offers hundreds more practice questions and many more mock tests. It contains new material, a significant revision of all the material previously published under the title *How to Pass Graduate Recruitment Tests,* and incorporates much of the material previously published under the Kogan Page title *How to Pass the Civil Service Qualifying Tests*.

Most of the exercises contained in this book have been used to assist groups of students to prepare for tests used by the most successful UK companies to recruit graduates and managers. I am grateful to these students for their helpful comments and suggestions. I also thank my colleagues at mbA training and Research and Development Ltd and Tol Bedford and Neil Scott of Recruitment and Assessment Services.

This bumper edition is dedicated to my children, Hope, Ella, Orlando and Allegra, and my wife Lorenza, who supported me during the evenings and weekends taken up by its production.

Chapter 1
Psychometric tests

Psychometric tests are multiple choice or short answer tests that are claimed to measure intelligence and ability. They are designed and developed by occupational psychologists and attempt to provide a numerical measurement of the extent to which an individual possesses a particular trait or set of traits. With these tests, the psychologist seeks to apply standardised scientific methods and statistical techniques.

In recruitment, psychometric tests are competitions. When they are used there are inevitably more applicants than opportunities and they are used to identify a few people for employment and to fail the rest. They are also tests of endurance. They comprise a series or battery of tests sat one after the other against tight time constraints over what can be a number of hours. When you leave the test centre you should feel worn out. I say 'should' because you have to apply yourself and really go for it if you are going to show your full potential and stand out from the crowd.

The tests can be undertaken either with a pen and paper or on a computer terminal.

Psychometric tests are used in a variety of applications. As well as an aid during recruitment, tests are used, for example, to select people for redundancy, diagnose an individual's strengths and weaknesses, allocate staff to particular tasks, select people for a place on a course of education and identify training need.

If used appropriately, tests can lead to better decisions regarding the potential of candidates. However, this is most likely to occur when tests are integrated into a recruitment process that includes a number of stages. The most commonly applied stages include:

● application form;

● test;

● interview;

● references.

Tests have been in use for many decades; however, there has been a significant rise in their use in recent years and this is a trend that is likely to continue.

The challenge of open and fair recruitment

From an employer's perspective, recruitment is a notoriously difficult business. Bad decisions and bad recruitment practice carry risks of damaging a business and legal challenge.

In an effort to make good recruitment decisions, employers turn to tools such as psychometric tests. In an effort to attract the best applicant most employers widely promote their vacancies. If they attract lots of applicants the cost and time it takes to scrutinise the large number of applicants can become a serious problem and it is often in these circumstances that the employer will turn to using psychometric tests.

These days employers are increasingly adopting a balanced view as to the contribution tests can make towards a fair and equitable selection process. It is increasingly common for tests to be viewed as predictors of likely job performance rather than some arbitrator of a fixed and unrevisable aptitude.

A welcome feature of this more balanced view is the fact that employers and occupational psychologists are moving away from abstract tests towards exercises more relevant to the workplace. Increasingly employers prefer exercises that test competencies and a vocabulary more closely associated with the demands of the job or are even taken directly from the role and workplace.

The downside of testing during recruitment

When a psychometric test is used for selection purposes the candidate will naturally try to get the best possible score and cover up any areas of weakness. In this situation the test author is working against the candidates and must produce a test that offers an objective assessment of the candidates' ability, despite the fact that the candidates are trying to distort the outcome. As a consequence, when a psychometric test is used for selection purposes, test security is of far greater importance. The impact of the effects of coaching on a candidate's score is also of far greater concern to the occupational psychologist.

To use a test as a valid predictor of potential job performance you first need a clear set of criteria against which to assess an individual. However, in the case of the majority of jobs it is very difficult to define an unambiguous set of criteria. Performance in most jobs is far too subjective a notion for a single set of indicators. Tests therefore risk attributing to the workplace too simplistic a set of performance indicators and in reality job performance is a complex tapestry of factors and influences that is very hard to quantify numerically.

Psychometric tests are scored and of course some candidates score higher than others. Unsurprisingly, there is a tendency among recruiters to assume that the higher a candidate scores, the greater the candidate's potential. Equally common is the tendency for the recruiter to be relieved that the poor-scoring candidate has been identified in such a dramatic and clear-cut way. The employer who relies too heavily on test scores and concludes from those scores that candidate x is the best and candidate y the second best applicant may find that in fact the best-scoring candidate does not have the best performance in the job. Most tests should be recognised as less than perfect. This is because, as we have already noted, job performance is often ill defined but also because the contents of most tests – the questions of which they are comprised – do not exactly measure the behaviour traits under investigation. They also inadvertently measure traits that are irrelevant to the post.

The scoring of tests is quite complex and they are accompanied by manuals and additional information against which a candidate's score should be interpreted. This information is used to compare a candidate's score against the scores of a sample of the wider population with broadly similar backgrounds to the applicant. Individuals responsible for the application of tests and the interpretation of the results should be trained to a level recommended by the British Psychological Society.

We have seen that an employer is likely to turn to tests when faced by a large number of applicants. However, the equitable selection of staff with psychometric tests is also made more difficult when faced by large numbers of applicants. This is because under such circumstances it becomes necessary to introduce cut-off points to reduce the number of candidates who pass through to the next stage. This is usually done by simply rejecting all candidates who score below a particular score or by fixing an upper limit to the number of applicants allowed through. Such cut-off points create problems because they result in the rejection of many candidates who have the potential to do the job. The fact that most tests are imperfect makes matters worse because they will inadvertently over-estimate the potential of some candidates who are allowed through to the next stage.

Test authors and employers go to considerable lengths to reassure us that their tests are objective and reliable and that they afford the selection of candidates with the potential to succeed in the given career or position. However, tests can only be viewed as objective and reliable when compared with other recruitment and selection methods, such as interviews, which are denounced as unreliable. When test authors talk about the objectivity of their tests they mean that the tests may be, for example, three times more reliable than interviews for predicting job performance. It is essential that you realise that three times more reliable than unreliable is quantifiably different from what is ordinarily meant by objective.

A lot of good candidates are put off by tests and many candidates fail to show their true potential. This means that in practice tests are wasteful in that they lead to the loss or discouragement of many candidates. In some circumstances an employer cannot afford to put off candidates before they have had the chance to demonstrate their potential. This is especially the case in industries suffering skill shortages or during periods of near full employment.

Some tests have been proven to discriminate unfairly and a responsible employer must monitor a test on a regular basis to guard against such discrimination.

Before an employer uses a test the recruiter should gather information from the authors of the test on:

- the reliability of the test;

- whether or not the test accurately identifies the attributes claimed;

- proof that the test does not unfairly disadvantage certain groups and so is lawful;

- evidence that the test has been used effectively in similar circumstances;

- how the test is evaluated and scored.

The suitability of a test needs to be regularly reviewed. In some fields of employment, such as information technology, the pace of change is so great that there is a real risk that a test quickly becomes ineffective.

While there are downsides associated with testing, there is no point in us getting too embroiled in a debate about the predicative value or otherwise of psychometric tests. Whether or not you or I consider them valid will not change the fact that many employers use them, and if you apply for a position and the recruitment process includes a test then you have little choice other than to take the test or withdraw your application.

Chapter 2
The maximum benefits of practice

The value of practice

If you face a psychometric test used to select people for employment then it is essential that you approach it with the right mental attitude. In particular, you must realise that your score can be improved by your own efforts.

Taking a psychometric test is not a matter of simply rolling up your sleeve and putting up with the discomfort of the needle while the scientist takes his or her sample. There is no ambiguity attached to a blood-type classification; there is very little prospect of it changing given different circumstances on the day on which the sample was taken. The objectivity of psychometric tests is quantifiably different. They are at best only indicators of potential. Had you not been suffering from a cold, had you been more familiar with the test conditions, been less nervous, better practised in mental arithmetic, not made that silly mistake... then you might have been classified differently. You might have passed something you otherwise failed.

Psychometric tests lack the certainty associated with the natural sciences. Accordingly, you, the subject, have considerable influence over the outcome according to the approach you take and the amount you prepare.

Everyone, if they practise, could improve their test score. The interesting question is whether or not you can improve your score sufficiently to pass something you would otherwise have failed.

Practice most benefits the candidate who is otherwise likely to fail by only a few marks; such people are sometimes referred to as 'near miss candidates'. The near miss candidate benefits most from practice because it is almost certain to ensure that s/he passes.

Candidates who have little or no experience of psychometric tests can through practice demonstrate a quite considerable improvement in their score. The biggest gains are achieved quickly and then the rate of improvement slows. The graph in Figure 2.1 illustrates the likely rate of improvement over 20 hours of practice for a candidate new to tests.

If you have recently left higher education, much of what you studied will have prepared you for employers' tests. As a result of this preparation it may be that you will not demonstrate the kind of improvement indicated in the graph. However, you may still benefit from practice. Psychometric tests usually require you to undertake exercises in both arithmetic and English usage, subjects which you may not have studied for some considerable time. The manner in which the questions are posed is also something likely to be unfamiliar and practice will help you to better realise the test demands. Finally, practice will allow you to deal with any nervousness and help you to avoid common mistakes.

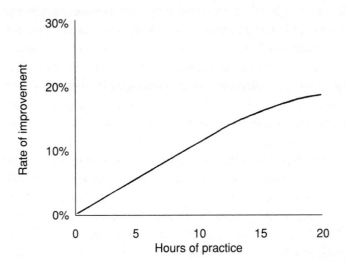

Figure 2.1

How much and what kind?

Practice will only work if the material on which you practise is as much like the questions in the real test as possible. The employer may have sent you a description of the test with examples of the type of question or have a Web site where you can sample questions. Study this document or Web site carefully and seek out practice material that closely resembles it.

It is best if you undertake two types of practice. You should:

1. Practise without time constraint and in an informal relaxed situation. The aim of this type of practice is that you realise the demands of the questions, understand how to approach them and gain speed and confidence in your ability to answer them.
2. Practise on realistic questions against a strict time constraint and under as realistic test conditions as you can.

The aim of these 'mock tests' is to get used to answering the type of questions under the conditions that exist in the real situation. This kind of practice helps you avoid mistakes that result from the pressures of the situation. You should aim to complete a minimum of three mock tests.

You may have to construct your own mock tests. To do this, seek out approximately 40 questions for each test; much of the practice material in this book may be suitable (sources of other suitable material are given in the list of further reading at the end of book). Allow yourself 45 seconds per question (in the real test it is unlikely that you will be able to complete all the questions in the time allowed). Make sure that all sections of the real test are represented. If, for example, the real test comprises sub-tests in maths, English usage and business judgement, make sure that your practice tests include all three types of question.

If your employer fails to provide you with a description of the test then telephone them and ask them to describe it. Ask, for example, how many sub-tests it involves, what are their titles, and who is the publisher.

If you are having any difficulties obtaining sufficient practice material or material of a certain type then by all means contact me via Kogan Page and if I know of any I will be more than happy to suggest sources.

Over a few days, aim to undertake a minimum of 12 hours' practice or, if you can obtain sufficient material, as much as 20 hours' practice. Ensure that you practise right up to the date of your test. Your schedule of work should look something like this:

1. Study the test description.
2. Seek out similar questions.

3. Go through practice questions at your own pace.
4. Set yourself a mock test against a strict time-limit.
5. Score and go over the mock test especially trying to understand where you went wrong.
6. Undertake more practice without time constraint – concentrate on your weaknesses.
7. Set yourself two further mock tests.

Practise only a little on the day before the test, and it is probably best if you don't practise on the day of the test itself.

A summary of research findings

A study of some of the literature on the effects of coaching highlighted the following findings. I summarise these findings in order that you can make your own assessment as to the likely benefit of practice and better understand the principal issues believed to determine the value of practice:

● Everyone can improve their score if they practise.

● Individuals with incomplete educational backgrounds are likely to benefit most from coaching.

● Those who have had no, or little, previous experience of tests show a rise about twice as large as those who have taken tests before.

● Improvements in scores are obtained by experiencing materials similar to those occurring in the real test.

● Practice with similar material under test conditions produces the best results.

● Most of the improvement is gained quickly; then the rate of improvement slows.

- The effect of coaching is highly specific in that there is little transfer to other types of test.

- Big individual differences are found in the effect of coaching.

- Greatest improvement in test performance is obtained not from coaching but from education.

- Graduates who have not studied maths or English language since their GCSEs can significantly improve their test scores through practice in these important types of sub-test.

Test strategies

Each test requires a slightly different test strategy. However, the following points about the approach you should adopt are universal, in that they apply to all psychometric tests.

The best-scoring candidates are the ones who arrive prepared. You should be fully aware of the demands of each sub-test before you attend on the day. Prior to the start of the test the test administrator or computer program will allow you to practise on a number of sample questions and explain to you the type of questions and the time allowed. You should be familiar with all this information. Your preparation should have included practice in all the types of question described.

Make sure you adopt the right approach during the test. The candidates that do best are the ones who look forward to the challenge of a test and the opportunity to demonstrate their abilities. They realise that they have nothing to lose if they do their best and 'go for it'. It is critical that you approach the test with confidence in your own abilities and preparation is the key to confidence.

Managing your time

We have seen how important it is to organise your time before the test. It is even more essential that you keep track of time during the test and manage how long you spend on any one question. You must ensure that you keep going right to the end. When it is applicable, take the last few minutes to go over checking your work.

You should aim to get right the balance between speed and accuracy. To do well you must work quickly whilst making the minimum of mistakes. This takes practice, especially as you may suffer anxiety or nerves during the test itself and as a consequence be prone to making more mistakes.

In multiple choice numerical questions, practise estimating answers. In some instances you can modify the sum to make it a more convenient, faster calculation and that way identify the correct answer from those suggested.

Everyone gets some answers wrong. It is better that you risk getting some questions wrong but attempt every question rather than double check every answer and be told you have run out of time before you have finished all the questions.

When you hit a difficult section or question don't lose heart. Just keep going – you may well find that you come next to a section or question in which you can excel.

Educated guessing is often worthwhile and worth practising. If you are unsure of the answer to a multiple choice question consider all the suggested answers and try ruling some out as wrong. This way you can reduce the number of suggested answers from which to guess and hopefully increase your chances of guessing correctly.

It is unlikely to help your score if you simply guess from the suggested answers in a random fashion. This is because many tests penalise wrong or unanswered questions. If, for example, a test offers four suggested answers to each question, then for every correct answer one point is awarded and for every four incorrect answers or unanswered questions a point is deducted.

To deal with penalties for wrong answers or no answers in a test you need to ensure that you manage your time to allow yourself to attempt every question and, when you do not know the answer, exercise educated guessing.

Chapter 3

Great candidate – except for the maths

Research indicates that one in six graduates lack confidence in the use of percentages, averages and the interpretation of tabulated data. Many lack a sufficient command of basic mental arithmetic. In many cases the problem is not innumeracy but a lack of recent knowledge, speed and accuracy.

These findings are hardly surprising given that a lot of graduates leave higher education having not studied maths since they were 16 years of age. If this research describes you, then you need to revise forgotten rules and build up your confidence, speed and accuracy. The only way you are going to do this is through practice. You may find it boring, painful even, but it has to be done if you want to demonstrate your full potential.

You need to be able to calculate both with and without a calculator. Some graduate tests allow the use of a calculator, which if allowed will be provided (possibly on screen). Note that their use is not permitted in all types of numeracy test and you cannot afford to assume that you will not need to work the sums manually. The exercises in this chapter should be undertaken without a calculator unless otherwise stated.

This section comprises four parts: a diagnostic exercise which is intended to identify the extent to which you need to practise, a glossary of the key terms, practice questions and mock tests.

For more practice, including practice in the interpretation of tabulated data, see Chapter 5.

Part 1

A diagnostic exercise

Allow yourself 25 minutes in which to complete the following 31 questions.

Addition

1. Find the sum of 79004, 24, 325 and 647.

    Answer

2. A company representative submits a travel claim form comprising the following:

Monday	105 miles	Thursday	144 miles
Tuesday	43 miles	Friday	12 miles
Wednesday	87 miles		

    What is the weekly total number of miles?

    Answer

3. A study of a family's expenditure found that each week on average they spent the following: £38.60 on food, £57.00 on accommodation, £14.20 on entertainment, £18.70 on heat and light and £9.00 on clothing. Excluding entertainment, what is the total spent?

    Answer

Subtraction

4. What is the difference between 373 and 3298?

Answer

5. Subtract 10303 from 60002.

Answer

6. The period sales figures for your department are illustrated in the table against your targets. How many unit sales must you make in the last period in order to achieve your overall target?

Period	Sales achieved	Targets
1	24	30
2	13	20
3	17	22
4	20	22
5	19	22
6		20

Answer

Multiplication

7. Multiply 35 by 68.

Answer

    ┌─────────────┐
    │   │
    └─────────────┘

8. A buyer agrees to pay 16 pence per unit for a lot which totals 103 units. What is the total cost of the purchase?

   Express your answer in pounds and pence.

Answer

    ┌─────────────┐
    │   │
    └─────────────┘

9. A machine can operate at 120 revolutions per minute. How many times will it rotate in half an hour?

Answer

    ┌─────────────┐
    │   │
    └─────────────┘

Division of whole numbers

10. Divide 185 by 5.

Answer

    ┌─────────────┐
    │   │
    └─────────────┘

11. Divide 2115 by 9.

Answer

12. British Gas sends out 27 million bills a year. They have made a deal with the Royal Mail who deliver the bills for £2,700,000. How much does it cost British Gas to deliver each bill?

Answer

Fractions

13. ⅓ + ⅔ + ⁷⁄₁₂ =

Answer

14. 3⅝ − 1¾ =

Answer

15. A railway wagon carries 20⅛ metric tonnes of flour in 12½ kg bags. How many bags of flour can be loaded onto the wagon? (Note that a metric tonne = 1,000 kg)

Answer

Decimals

16. Add 3.36 and 4.60 and then deduct 2.3 from the total.

Answer

17. Convert ⅟₁₆ into decimals.

Answer

18. Multiply 3.7 by 4.83.

Answer

Ratios

19. Parked in a street there are 14 cars and 4 motor cycles. What is the ratio of cars to motor cycles?

Answer

20. The ratio of car drivers to cyclists in a city is found to be 4:1. How many cyclists were counted in the survey if the sample totalled 2,500?

Answer

21. A fuel mixture comprises the ratio 14 parts fuel to 1 part oil. How much oil will be present in 9 litres of fuel mixture? (Note there are 100 cl in 1 litre.)

Answer

Averages

22. Find the average of 7,12,14 and 16.

Answer

23. A shop sold 3 watches at £16, a ring at £30 and 4 travelling alarm clocks at £9 each. What was the average sale price?

Answer

24. To pass an exam you have to average 60 marks across four papers. After three papers a candidate's score is averaging 52. What mark must the candidate achieve in the final paper in order to pass the exam?

Answer

Percentages

25. Find 43% of £5.

Answer

26. A pair of shoes is normally priced at £37. What will be the sale price if a 25% discount is offered?

Answer

27. An invoice totals £5,000 and includes VAT at 17.5%. How much was the invoice made out for excluding VAT? Round your answer up to the nearest penny.

Answer

Basic algebra

28. A receiver has to share a sum of money between three creditors. Creditor X is to receive £1,000 more than creditor Y. Creditor Z is to receive three times as much as creditor Y. Devise a linear equation which allows you to establish that creditor X will receive £1,600 if creditor Z is paid £1,800.

Answer

29. A shop buys watches for £10 and sells them for £16. What is the percentage gross profit?

Answer

Sequencing

30. 2, 5, 8, 11, ?, 17.

Answer

[   ]

31. 3, 4, 12, 48, ?

Answer

[   ]

You will find the answers to this exercise at the end of the chapter. Mark your answers and use the result to establish in which types of question you need to undertake further practice.

If you failed to complete the exercise in the time allowed you need more practice in order to build up your speed.

Make use of the glossary of terms to obtain explanations if you require them. If you find the glossary too brief, then both libraries and bookshops should have a good selection of numeracy textbooks in which you will find fuller explanations.

Part 2

Glossary

Key terms and methods

If it is some years since you studied mathematics, then it is important that you remind yourself of the meanings of key terms and methods.

The following glossary of terms is intended only as a reminder. The suggested methods are by no means the only way to work the calculations. If you rely on another method then it is probably best if you stick with it.

Make sure that you can operate quickly, accurately and with confidence the following rules and methods.

Addition

If the numbers have the same sign (positive or negative) then you add them together and use the same sign in the number. If the numbers have different signs then apply the rule that + - is the same as -. For example:

$$2 + -6 = -4$$
$$16 + -2 = 14$$

If you subtract a smaller number from a larger one the answer will be positive. If you subtract a large number from a smaller one the result will be negative.

Angle

Angles are measured in degrees and record the amount of turn. A right angle has 90 degrees, an obtuse angle is greater that 90 but less than 180 degrees and a reflex angle is greater than 180 degrees. Angles on a straight line add up to 180 degrees, while angles from a point add up to 360 degrees.

Area

Area is a two-dimensional measurement. To work out the area of a square you multiply the length of one side by itself. All areas are measured in squares, eg square centimetres. To establish the area of a rectangle multiply length by width. The area occupied by a triangle is established by multiplying its height by half the length of its base line.

Average

The average or arithmetic mean is found by adding up all the figures and dividing the total by the number of figures. 'Average' differs from 'Mode', the item of data which occurs the most often, and 'Median', the figure or item of data which is in the middle once all the items have been put into a specific order.

Bar chart

A visual representation of data which allows the viewer to make comparisons between the frequency or quantity of items. It is used when the horizontal scale is simply a list. The bars are of equal width; the frequency or quantity is illustrated by the height of the bar.

Brackets

When there appear several ways in which to proceed with a calculation, to ensure the calculation proceeds in the correct order the items to be calculated first are enclosed within brackets. Work out the parts in brackets first. Brackets are sometimes referred to as a 'first priority'. A second priority is multiplication and division which must be done before the third priority – addition and subtraction.

Circle

The circumference of a circle is the outer edge and is calculated with the equation Pi × diameter. A cord is any straight line drawn from one part of the circumference to another. When a circle has a cord drawn on it, the circle is divided into two segments. A straight line taken from the circumference to the centre is called the radius; and a straight line taken from one part of the circumference to another, which passes through the centre, is called the diameter. The area of a circle is calculated with the equation Pi × the square of its radius.

Congruent

If shapes, for example squares or triangles, have the same angle and all the lengths are the same, they are said to be congruent. Shapes are said to be similar if the angles are the same and the ratio of all the corresponding lengths is equal.

Cube

A cube has six square faces at right angles to each other. The cube of a number is established if the number is multiplied by itself twice: for example, the cube of $5 = 5 \times 5 \times 5$ (answer 125). The cube root of 125 is therefore 5. The sign for cube root is $\sqrt[3]{}$.

Decimal number

A decimal number has a decimal point. The point serves to separate the whole number from the decimal fraction. Some decimals are recurring. Decimal places after the point represent, respectively, tenths, hundredths, thousandths, and so on.

Distance

To calculate distance, multiply rate of travel by time.

Division

It is unusual in a psychometric test to have to undertake long division, especially if the sum is awkward. Some test publishers, however, may want to establish if you are aware of short cuts and patterns in mathematics. For this reason it is worth looking to see if the question has been formed so as to test, for example, whether you realise one of the following:

● A number is divisible by 2 if the last digit is even.

● A number is divisible by 5 if its last digit is either 5 or 0 and by 10 if its last digit is 0 (to divide by 10 simply take off the 0).

● A number is divisible by 3 if the sum of its digits is divisible by 3.

● A number is divisible by 9 if the sum of its digits is divisible by 9.

- A number is divisible by 4 if the number formed by the last two digits is divisible by 4.

- A number is divisible by 8 if the number formed by the last three digits is divisible by 8.

- A number is divisible by 6 if it is also divisible by both 2 and 3.

Exponent

An exponent is the power to which something has been raised. For example, the exponent is 2 in the term 10 to the power of 2 and this is expressed as 10^2.

Factor

A factor is a whole number that will divide into another number exactly. The factors of, for example, 8 are 1, 2, 4 and 8.

Factorise

If you factorise an equation or mathematical expression you separate it into bracketed parts which, if multiplied together, will give that expression.

Fractions

A fraction is a part of a whole number. You need to be able to work with both decimal and vulgar fractions. Decimal fractions are described in the entry entitled 'decimal number'. Vulgar fractions use whole numbers one above the other. The lower number is called the denominator and the upper number is called the numerator. An improper fraction is one where the numerator is bigger than the denominator.

Fractions can be changed to another equivalent fraction and still have the same value. You should always finish a calculation by expressing a fraction in its lowest term.

To change a fraction to a lower equivalent you look to divide both the numerator and denominator by the same number. This is called cancelling. If the number is even you can always divide by 2. Sometimes you cancel more than once before you arrive at the lowest equivalent.

To add or subtract fractions you need to ensure that all the denominators are the same. In the example:

$$\frac{1}{2} + \frac{3}{8} = ?$$

You find the common denominator which is 8 and convert to eighths =

$$\frac{4}{8} + \frac{3}{8} \quad \text{The answer is} \quad \frac{7}{8}$$

To multiply fractions make sure that any mixed numbers (whole numbers and fractions) are converted into improper fractions and then multiply all the numerators and all the denominators together.

To divide fractions change any mixed numbers into improper fractions and then turn the fractions upside down (invert them) and multiply.

Frequency

Frequency is the number of times an event occurs.

Generalise

If we find a pattern and express it using algebraic expressions we are said to have generalised it.

Graph

A graph is a diagram comprising two reference lines, called axes, at right angles to each other. A scale is marked along each axis. Graphs are used to show a relationship between two quantities. Before you begin to calculate with figures taken from a graph take care to establish that the units are comparable and that you are looking in the correct column or line. See X and Y.

Histogram

A histogram is similar to a bar chart except that it is the areas of the bars that represent the frequency or quantity rather than the length of the bars.

Inequalities

These are signs used to indicate relative size. Examples you must understand are:

> means greater than
< means less than

Interest: compound and simple

You may well face questions that require you to work out simple or, more likely, compound interest.

Simple interest involves a quantity of money and a rate of interest. You simply multiply the amount of money by the rate of interest and divide by 100 to establish the interest earned.

Compound interest is the type most banks offer. The interest is added to the amount saved and you then receive interest on both the amount saved and the interest earned. The total compound interest can be roughly estimated by using the following formula, which if applied will save time. Try it and decide its value for yourself:

Final amount = $P \times (R/100)N + P$

where: P = Amount initially invested
R = Percentage rate of interest
N = Number of years investment made

Mean, Median and Mode

See Average.

Multiplication

Make sure the units of each number are underneath each other. To multiply any whole number by 10, 100, 1,000 and so on simply add a 0 in the case of multiplying by 10, two 0s in the case of 100, etc.

To multiply decimals, ignore the decimal point and proceed as if the numbers were whole. When you have finished multiplying, count for each decimal how many figures (including 0s) there are to the right of the decimal point and add them together. The total gives you the number of decimal figures to the right of the point you must have in your answer.

Percentage

Percentage is a way of describing parts of a whole. One per cent (1%) represents one out of a hundred. To calculate, for example, 25% of 300 we calculate:

$$300 \times {}^{25}\!/_{100} = 75$$

Percentage as fractions. A percentage is a fraction with a denominator of 100. To express a percentage as a fraction, all you need do is express it as its lowest term.

Percentage as decimals. To change a percentage into a decimal, all you need do is divide it by 100. You can do this by moving the decimal point 2 places towards the left.

Changing fractions and decimals into percentages. Multiply by 100.

Percentage decrease and increase. To work out a percentage decrease or increase you compare the decrease or increase with the original amount.

If the amount is to be decreased by, for example, 20% then we need to calculate 100 – 20 = 80% of the total. Likewise, if we want to increase an amount by, say, 10% we have to calculate 10% of the original amount.

To work out 80% of £14 we use the following method:

$$\frac{80}{100} \times 14 = £11.20$$

Value added tax and profit and loss

Test questions of percentage are often concerned with value added tax (VAT) or profit and loss.

VAT

Ensure that you are able to work out the amount of VAT to be charged and the amount of VAT contained in an inclusive sum. The first of these is easy. To work out the VAT contained in a total, use the following method:

Treat the inclusive sum as 100% + the percentage rate of VAT. Then work out 100% of the total.

You can also find VAT by multiplying the total, inclusive of VAT at 17.5%, by $\frac{7}{47}$.

Profit and loss

We buy goods at one price and sell them at another. Test questions often expect profit and loss to be expressed as a percentage. The way to approach these questions is as follows:

1. Work out the cash profit or loss.
2. Express this as a fraction of the original (buying) price.
3. Convert this fraction to a percentage.

Pi

The sign for Pi is π and is found by dividing the circumference of a circle by its diameter.

Pictograms

A pictogram is a representation of information which uses pictures to denote the frequency or quantity.

Pie chart

A pie chart divides a circle into sectors the size of which represents a portion of the whole.

Powers

See Exponent.

Priorities

See Brackets.

Probability

The likelihood of an event happening can be expressed. The comparison can be shown as, for example, a fraction, percentage or ratio (see below). If something is considered impossible then the probability is 0, if there is an even chance it is expressed as ½ and if an event is a certainty it is expressed as 1. The probability of a dice being rolled and it coming to rest with the number 3 at the top is ⅙.

Quartiles

If you have a graph demonstrating the cumulative frequency of a quantity, it may be divided into equal quarters and these are called quartiles of a distribution. Quartiles are added to the graph by dividing the total frequency into equal groups. You have an upper and lower quartile and the median.

Ratio

Ratio is a comparison of quantities. Like fractions, they can be simplified or cancelled down. For example, if you are told that the ratio between men and women is 25:50 this can be simplified to 1:2.

Running totals or cumulative frequency

A running total allows you to realise the total to date and find out the median and the quartiles of distribution. If drawn on a graph, the cumulative frequency will form a distinctive curve known as the ogive.

Sequence tests

For many candidates sequencing tests offer the chance to show considerable improvement through practice. They really are a lot easier than they at first seem.

A sequence is offered with one of the set missing which you have to identify. The sequence can start and end at any point. The most common types are as follows:

Addition

The sequence for adding the number 8 can be presented as:

480, 488, 504, 512, 520, 528, and so on.

Subtraction

If a sequence is decreasing from left to right it may be the result of subtraction. Subtraction of the figure 6 can be illustrated as follows:

540, 534, 528, 522, 516, 510, 504.

Multiplication

This common type of sequence is constructed as a result of multiplying the same number each time. The sequence derived by the multiplication of 3 is, for example, as follows:

2, 6, 18, 54, 162, 486.

Division

In a way similar to multiplication, a sequence can be constructed as a result of division. For example, division by 5 each time produces the following sequence:

37500, 7500, 1500, 300, 60.

Add two previous terms

This type of sequence is generated by adding the two previous numbers to obtain the next in the series. For example:

1, 4, 5, 9, 14, 23, 37.

Multiply two previous numbers

Related to the previous example, this sequence is obtained by multiplying the two previous digits:

3, 4, 12, 48, 576.

Alternating signs

A number may have either a positive or a negative sign and the sign of the numbers which make up a sequence may be alternated in an attempt to make it less recognisable. For example:

2, –4, 8, –16, 32, –64, 128.

Addition of two common sequences

Take the sequence:

1, 2, 4, 7, 11, 16, 22, 29, 37, 46.

It is produced by adding a term from the sequence 1, 2, 3, 4, 5, 6, 7, 8, 9 to the previous number. To get 2 we add 1 to the first term, to get 4 we add 2 to 2, to get 7 we add 3 to 4, and so on. This type of sequence is produced as a result of adding a number to the first term to get the second but adding a different number to get the fourth. You work out what number to add each time because they belong to another sequence.

Hidden series

Sometimes the test author will try to hide a sequence by presenting it in a misleading manner. For example:

123, 456, 789, 101, 112, 131, 415, 161, 718.

All the test author has done in this instance is present the most common sequence of all in a different way. The sequence is the numbers 1–18.

Sequences worth remembering

The following sequences come up often and are worth committing to memory if they are not familiar:

The power of 2 sequence	2, 4, 8, 16, 32, 64, 128, 256
The power of 3 sequence	3, 9, 27, 81, 243, 729
The square of numbers	1, 4, 9, 16, 25, 36, 49, 64, 81, 100
A sequence of factors	1, 2, 6, 24, 120, 720
The cubes of numbers	1, 8, 27, 64, 125, 216
The power of 4 sequence	4, 16, 64, 256, 1024
The sequence of prime numbers	1, 2, 3, 5, 7, 11, 13, 17, 19, 23, 29

Set

A set is a collection or class of items that have something in common. In mathematics a set is indicated by this type of bracket { }. An example of a set (in this case a finite set) is the set of positive numbers under 10 – {1 2 3 4 5 6 7 8 9 10}.

Square root

The square root of a number is that number which, if multiplied by itself, would give your original number. For example, the square root of 25 is 5 because $5 \times 5 = 25$. Every number has both a positive and a negative square root. The square roots of 25 are both 5 and –5 (remember, if two minus numbers are multiplied, they equal a positive).

Subtraction

There are two widely practised methods of subtraction. I will illustrate them with the following example:

$$\begin{array}{r} 93 \\ -27 \\ \hline 66 \end{array}$$

In method A, you would borrow 10 from the 9 to make the 3 = 13; the 9 would then become an 8. In method B, we would again add 10 to the 3 to make it 13 but this time we would also add 10 to the 2 on the bottom line to make it 3.

Stick with whichever method you were taught and practise to make sure you are accurate and quick.

Triangle

The sum of the inside angles of a triangle is always 180 degrees. An equilateral triangle is one with three equal sides and three equal angles, all 60 degrees. A right-angle triangle is one with a right angle. An isosceles triangle is one with two equal sides and two equal angles.

Volume

Volume is the measurement of the three-dimensional space occupied by a solid. It is quantifiable in cubic measurement, for example cubic metres.

There are formulae for finding volume in all the regular shapes. To find the volume of a box, for instance, you multiply length by breadth by height. To find the volume of shapes which have vertical sides of equal lengths, for example, a cylinder or a triangular prism, you multiply the area of the base by the height.

Whole numbers

Examples of whole numbers are 0,1 2, 3, 4, and so on. A whole number that is divisible by 2 is called an even number. A number not divisible by 2 is an odd number. Note that a number is said to be divisible only if a second number divides into it without any remainder.

X and Y

The horizontal (X) and vertical (Y) axes on a two-dimensional graph are referred to as the X and Y axes.

Part 3

Practice questions

1. A till roll is 10 metres long while the average till receipt is 8 cm long. How many customers can be served before the till roll needs to be changed?

    Answer

2. A store serves 6,000 customers a day. Given that the average till receipt is 8 cm long and a till roll is 10 metres long, how many till rolls will be used each day?

    Answer

3. A household's water bill is £240 and is charged at 15 pence a gallon. How many gallons of water does the household use?

    Answer

4. A household's water bill of £240 is to increase by 12%. What will be the new total?

Answer

5. If a water bill of £240 includes VAT at 17.5%, how much VAT will be paid? Express your answer to the nearest whole penny.

Answer

6. The pages of a novel have on average 50 lines comprising 12 words. If in total there are 175 pages, how many words does the novel contain?

Answer

7. A cyclist averages 7.5 miles an hour on level ground but only 4.5 miles an hour going uphill. If the ratio between flat ground and hills is 1:3, what is the cyclist's average mph over 60 miles?

Answer

8. A publisher must sell 20,000 books at an average unit cost of £7.60 to break even. If salaries account for 40% of expenditure, how much is the wages bill?

    Answer

9. A box of chocolates comprises 12 chocolates and weighs ¾ of a kilogram. If the packaging weighs ⅕ of the total, how much does each chocolate weigh? Express your answer as a fraction of a pound.

    Answer

10. A garage discovered that ½ of their customers bought French cars, ⅓ German cars and ⅙ (20) American cars. How many customers did the garage have?

    Answer

11. How much is ⅗ of £750?

    Answer

12. One-half of the turnover of a business is spent on salaries, one-third on production and distribution. After setting aside £10,000 for marketing, there is £23,000 left. How much is the total turnover?

Answer

13. In a sale goods were advertised at ¼ of their marked price. What was the total sales price for:

   A calculator marked price £5.90?
   A book marked price £17.30?
   Jeans marked price £44.00?

Answer

14. To travel to work a woman spends 70 pence on a bus fare and 120 pence on a train fare. She spends the same amount on the way home. In a normal working week, how much would she save if she bought a travel pass at £14.50?

Answer

15. A man purchased a lottery ticket each week (52 weeks a year) for six years. He worked out that he would have to win £624 to recoup his money. How much did each ticket cost?

Answer

16. A full price ticket to Liverpool costs £84. If you travel after 9.30 the cost drops to £32. What percentage saving does this represent?

Answer

17. There are only 24 women out of a total workforce of 1,200 in an engineering company. What is the ratio of female to male employees?

Answer

18. From an initial fee of £600 a company had to credit back to the customer £96 to cover a dry-cleaning bill. What is the % refund?

Answer

19. Find the compound interest on £2,000 invested for 3 years at 5% per annum (pa).

Answer

[ ]

20. A 16 kg sack of potatoes costs £4.50. How much does a kilogram of potatoes cost? Express your answer to the nearest whole penny.

Answer

[ ]

21. A bank offers 6% pa interest calculated annually. Another offers 10% pa compound interest calculated every six months. What is the difference paid at the end of the year on a deposit of £1,000?

Answer

[ ]

22. A new ship is 300 feet long and its plans are on a scale of 1:200. How long is the ship as it is represented on the plans?

Answer

[ ]

23. An investment of £10,000 earns interest at 6% pa fixed for a 5-year period. How much will the total investment with interest amount to at the end of the 5-year period?

Answer

24. A business loan of £2,000 is to have interest charged at 20% pa. How much will the monthly repayments be if both the interest and loan are to be repaid in one year?

Answer

25. The interest on a car loan of £3,000 is to be charged at 15% pa. How much will the monthly repayments be if both the loan and interest are to be repaid in 24 months? Express your answer to the nearest penny.

Answer

26. A box of 100 pens is bought for £5 and sold for 8 pence each. What is the percentage profit?

Answer

27. A table was sold for £280 at a 20% loss. What was the buying price?

Answer

28. A watch costs £9.00 plus VAT which is charged at 17.5%. What is the total price to be paid?

Answer

29. An estimate is made for £2,000 plus VAT (at 17.5%) for the preparation of a business plan. How much VAT is to be paid?

Answer

30. A restaurant bill totals £110.00 inclusive of VAT and a service charge. VAT was charged at 17.5% after a service charge of 10% was levied. How much was the bill excluding the VAT and service charge? Express your answer to the nearest penny.

Answer

31. A photocopier service contract costs £40 a month excluding VAT (at 17.5%). How much VAT is paid in 12 months?

Answer

32. A cooker is sold for £800 inclusive of VAT which is charged at 17.5%. How much did the cooker cost excluding VAT?

Answer

33. Divide £50 into the ratio of 3:2.

Answer

34. Components A, B and C are ordered in the ratio 1:5:4. How many of each are included in an order which totals 1,000 components?

Answer

35. In some areas in the United Kingdom male unemployment is as high as 30% of the total economically active population. Express this level of unemployment as a ratio.

Answer

[   ]

36. On a housing estate 60% of the unemployed were found to have last worked in the construction industry, while 24% last worked in the public service sector and 16% last worked in retail and distribution. Express these quantities as a ratio.

Answer

[   ]

37. The ratio between unemployed graduates to unemployed people without any kind of qualification is 1:8. If 30 unemployed graduates are found to use a Job Centre, how many unemployed people with no qualification might be expected to attend?

Answer

[   ]

38. A woman earns £13,000 and has a tax-free single person's allowance of £2,800. How much tax would she pay on her taxable earnings (assume the rate of tax is 24%).

Answer

39. A man earns £200 a week. He pays tax at 24% on all his earnings over his annual tax-free allowance of £2,300. How much tax does he pay each week? Express your answer to the nearest penny.

Answer

40. If tax is charged at 24%, how much is payable on a taxable income of £10,000?

Answer

41. A car travels 70 miles in 2½ hours. What is its average speed?

Answer

42. A train travels at an average speed of 110 mph. How long does it take to travel 385 miles?

Answer

43. A yacht averages 4 nautical miles an hour but the tide is running against it at one knot. How long will the yacht take to reach a harbour 1.5 nautical miles away? (Note that 1 knot = 1 nautical mile an hour.)

Answer

44. The initial price on an item was £99 but it was reduced in a sale by 10%. After a week a further 10% discount was made on the new price. What was the eventual asking price?

Answer

45. A machine produces 130 nuts in 10 minutes. A second machine produces 264 nuts in 12 minutes. How long would it take the two machines running simultaneously to produce 700 nuts?

Answer

46. A total of 5,000 copies of a book were sold: 60% were sold at 50% discount, 20% were sold at 30% discount while the remainder were sold at the cover price of £6.99. What was the total revenue?

Answer

47. In an election the Yellow Party candidate received ½ as many votes as the Red Party candidate. The Red Party candidate received ⅓ more votes than the candidate from the Blue Party. In total, 10,000 people voted for the Blue Party candidate. How many votes did the Yellow Party candidate receive?

Answer

48. In a sample of 220, 5% were positive. In a second sample of 120, 10% were positive. What was the combined number of positive responses?

Answer

49. A printer prints 20 characters a second and is 4 times as fast as the average printer. If the average printer is 5 times as fast as Jill the copy typist, how many characters can Jill type a second?

Answer

50. After paying 24% tax on all income over £2,300, a person has a net income of £12,000. What was the income before tax?

Answer

Find the missing numbers in the following sequences:

51.   2, 5, 11, ?, 17, 20

52.   504, 512, 520, ? , 536

53.   540, 534, 528, 522, 516, 510, ?

54.   ?, 6, 18, 54, 162, 486

55.   37500, 7500, ?, 300, 60

56.   1, 4, ?, 9, 14, 23, 37

57.   2, –4, 8, –16, 32, –64, ?

58.   123, 456, 789, 101, 112, ?

59.   3, 9, 27, 81, ?, 729

60.   1, 8, 27, 64, 125, ?

You will find the answers to these practice questions at the end of the chapter.

Part 4

Mock tests

Mock test 1

The test that begins over the page comprises 23 numerical tasks for which you are allowed 20 minutes. So you need to complete each question in just over 50 seconds. Six possible answers are offered to each question and labelled alphabetically A, B, C, D, E, F. Only one of the suggested answers is correct. You are required to work out which of the six suggested answers is correct and enter the corresponding letter in the answer box.

Do not use a calculator or other mechanical aid.

Do look at the suggested answers to see if you can save time by estimating the answers.

When it helps, round sums up or down to more convenient amounts. If you cannot work out a question, practise educated guessing.

Make a note of the time and then turn the page and begin the mock test.

1. The plane is due to depart at 14.15 hours. You are required to check in one and a half hours before departure and need to allow two hours to travel to the airport. What time would you need to leave your house?

A	B	C	D	E	F
11.5	9.45	10.45	Noon	11.45	10.15

2. In 1995, 60 per cent of graduates were found to be poor at the interpretation of information when it was presented numerically. If there were 2,200 graduates that year, how many were able to interpret this kind of information?

A	B	C	D	E	F
1,320	1,100	2,200	1,400	880	1,000

3. A factory worker worked 37.5 hours a week. How many hours did she work over a 12-week period?

A	B	C	D	E	F
450	300	440	296	375	950

4. An office worker was required to keep a time sheet detailing how long it took to undertake each task. Excluding lunch, what was the total time taken to complete all the following tasks?

Franking mail	20 minutes
Amending computer files	45 minutes
Answering the telephone	70 minutes
Lunch	30 minutes

A	B	C	D	E	F
2½ hours	2 hours 5 minutes	2 hours	1¾ hours	2¼ hours	1½ hours

5. A survey in a café found that a quarter of all customers took sugar and eight took sweetener. What fraction of customers took no sugar or sweetener?

A	B	C	D	E	F
¾	⁹⁄₁₆	⅜	⅝	½	¹⁄₂₀

6. A survey found that 3/16ths of women said that they would always shop at a complex that offered baby changing facilities; 5/8ths said that they thought it advantageous if a complex offered this service, while the remaining 75 respondents indicated that they thought it made no difference. What number of women said they thought the service advantageous?

A	B	C	D	E	F
25	250	150	50	125	175

7. If a machine is designed to rotate 300 times a minute, how many rotations does it perform in an hour?

A	B	C	D	E	F
18 million	9,000	9 million	180,000	18,000	90,000

8. If the fastest student in the class can type at 30 words a minute, while the slowest can only manage 20 words, what would be the time difference between them if they undertook to input a document comprising 3,000 words?

A	B	C	D	E	F
50 minutes	1 hour	45 minutes	1¼ hours	90 minutes	100 minutes

9. An architect designed a long, sweeping staircase which was a total of 16 metres in length. He specified that the staircase was to have 48 steps. Approximately, what was the length of each step?

A	B	C	D	E	F
½ metre	200 cm	¼ metre	300 cm	400 cm	⅓ metre

10. It was recommended that the photocopier was serviced every half a million copies and on average it was used to undertake 70,000 copies a month. How many months should pass between services?

A	B	C	D	E	F
3	8	6	7	9	4

11. The head teacher of a school realised that he had overspent on the wages by 5 per cent. If the monthly total was supposed to be kept under £21,000, how much had been overspent?

A	B	C	D	E	F
£1,500	£950	£1,050	£1,175	£1,000	£700

12. A ship's engine was found to achieve a speed of 9 knots at 2,700 revolutions. How many extra revolutions would you expect to be required if the captain asked to increase the speed to 9.5 knots?

A	B	C	D	E	F
600	400	300	150	450	200

13. Your office used 16 stamps at 25 pence each and 42 stamps at 19 pence each. What was the total postage bill?

A	B	C	D	E	F
£13.73	£11.98	£13.29	£11.60	£13.54	£11.73

14. Your office referred 22 files to storage over a three-month period and they took up just over 4 metres of shelving. At that rate, how long would you expect it to take before your stored files occupied a kilometre of shelf space (Answers are expressed in whole years.)

A	B	C	D	E	F
12 years	10 years	62 years	90 years	83 years	50 years

15. From what time should you book the conference room if the delegates' train arrives at 13.00 hours, the station is approximately 15 minutes away and you expect them to lunch with the Minister for two hours before the seminar begins?

A	B	C	D	E	F
Noon	4.00 pm	1.30 pm	3.15 pm	2.00 pm	2.45 pm

16. The photocopier operates at 45 copies a minute. How many minutes will it take to duplicate 1,100 copies?

A	B	C	D	E	F
20	50	21	55	24	19

17. Three departments decided to share equally the cost of a new piece of equipment. The bill totalled £3,780. How much did each department have to contribute?

A	B	C	D	E	F
£1,260	£260	£2,260	£1,890	£2,890	£890

18. A metre of rope cost 29 pence. How much would 120 metres cost?

A	B	C	D	E	F
£29.29	£36.50	£34.80	£37.10	£29.10	£29.00

19. If 350 people entered a competition and each paid £1.20, how much would remain if the organiser had to spend a total of £200 on prizes?

A	B	C	D	E	F
£220.20	£220	£22.40	£218.80	£217.60	£215.20

20. A pack of 8 pots of liquid correction fluid costs £7.68. What is the cost of each pot?

A	B	C	D	E	F
130p	85p	76.3p	109p	18p	96p

21. Most telephone calls were received between 10.00 and 11.00 am, which is three times as many as the 150 calls received between 3.00 and 4.00 pm. On average, how many calls a minute were received during the busiest hour?

A	B	C	D	E	F
6	150	7½	2½	16	450

22. A 50-gram item costs 25 pence to post. At the same rate, how much would you expect to pay to post an item that weighed a kilo?

    A   B   C   D   E   F
    £15   £150   £200   £500   £20   £5

23. If tax on a £150 television set is £22.50, how much tax is paid on a television which costs £1,050?

    A   B   C   D   E   F
    £157.50 £210.00 £183.75 £105.00 £73.50   £52.50

End of Mock test 1

You will find the answers to this mock test at the end of the chapter.

Mock test 2

Over the page you will find 26 practice sequencing questions. In each sequence one entry has been replaced with 'XX'. Alongside each question is a box where you must mark your answer.

Always enter two digits in your answer. If the answer is a single figure, enter a zero in front of it (eg 05).

Allow yourself 20 minutes to complete the test.

Do not turn over the page until you are ready to start.

1. 20 33 46 XX 72

0	[ ]	0	[ ]
1	[ ]	1	[ ]
2	[ ]	2	[ ]
3	[ ]	3	[ ]
4	[ ]	4	[ ]
5	[ ]	5	[ ]
6	[ ]	6	[ ]
7	[ ]	7	[ ]
8	[ ]	8	[ ]
9	[ ]	9	[ ]

2. 6 9 XX 15 18

0	[ ]	0	[ ]
1	[ ]	1	[ ]
2	[ ]	2	[ ]
3	[ ]	3	[ ]
4	[ ]	4	[ ]
5	[ ]	5	[ ]
6	[ ]	6	[ ]
7	[ ]	7	[ ]
8	[ ]	8	[ ]
9	[ ]	9	[ ]

3.   61   122   183   2XX   305

0	[ ]		0	[ ]
1	[ ]		1	[ ]
2	[ ]		2	[ ]
3	[ ]		3	[ ]
4	[ ]		4	[ ]
5	[ ]		5	[ ]
6	[ ]		6	[ ]
7	[ ]		7	[ ]
8	[ ]		8	[ ]
9	[ ]		9	[ ]

4.   1027   963   8XX   835

0	[ ]		0	[ ]
1	[ ]		1	[ ]
2	[ ]		2	[ ]
3	[ ]		3	[ ]
4	[ ]		4	[ ]
5	[ ]		5	[ ]
6	[ ]		6	[ ]
7	[ ]		7	[ ]
8	[ ]		8	[ ]
9	[ ]		9	[ ]

5. 5 10 20 XX 80

0	[	]	0	[	]
1	[	]	1	[	]
2	[	]	2	[	]
3	[	]	3	[	]
4	[	]	4	[	]
5	[	]	5	[	]
6	[	]	6	[	]
7	[	]	7	[	]
8	[	]	8	[	]
9	[	]	9	[	]

6. 3 12 48 1XX 768

0	[	]	0	[	]
1	[	]	1	[	]
2	[	]	2	[	]
3	[	]	3	[	]
4	[	]	4	[	]
5	[	]	5	[	]
6	[	]	6	[	]
7	[	]	7	[	]
8	[	]	8	[	]
9	[	]	9	[	]

7.   2 6 18 54 1XX

0	[ ]	0	[ ]
1	[ ]	1	[ ]
2	[ ]	2	[ ]
3	[ ]	3	[ ]
4	[ ]	4	[ ]
5	[ ]	5	[ ]
6	[ ]	6	[ ]
7	[ ]	7	[ ]
8	[ ]	8	[ ]
9	[ ]	9	[ ]

8.   3 5 7 XX 13 15

0	[ ]	0	[ ]
1	[ ]	1	[ ]
2	[ ]	2	[ ]
3	[ ]	3	[ ]
4	[ ]	4	[ ]
5	[ ]	5	[ ]
6	[ ]	6	[ ]
7	[ ]	7	[ ]
8	[ ]	8	[ ]
9	[ ]	9	[ ]

9. 64 32 16 XX 4 2 1

0	[ ]	0	[ ]
1	[ ]	1	[ ]
2	[ ]	2	[ ]
3	[ ]	3	[ ]
4	[ ]	4	[ ]
5	[ ]	5	[ ]
6	[ ]	6	[ ]
7	[ ]	7	[ ]
8	[ ]	8	[ ]
9	[ ]	9	[ ]

10. 4 6 8 XX 12 14 16

0	[ ]	0	[ ]
1	[ ]	1	[ ]
2	[ ]	2	[ ]
3	[ ]	3	[ ]
4	[ ]	4	[ ]
5	[ ]	5	[ ]
6	[ ]	6	[ ]
7	[ ]	7	[ ]
8	[ ]	8	[ ]
9	[ ]	9	[ ]

11. 20 18 16 14 XX 14 16 18 20

0	[ ]	0	[ ]
1	[ ]	1	[ ]
2	[ ]	2	[ ]
3	[ ]	3	[ ]
4	[ ]	4	[ ]
5	[ ]	5	[ ]
6	[ ]	6	[ ]
7	[ ]	7	[ ]
8	[ ]	8	[ ]
9	[ ]	9	[ ]

12. 2 3 5 6 XX 9 11 12 14

0	[ ]	0	[ ]
1	[ ]	1	[ ]
2	[ ]	2	[ ]
3	[ ]	3	[ ]
4	[ ]	4	[ ]
5	[ ]	5	[ ]
6	[ ]	6	[ ]
7	[ ]	7	[ ]
8	[ ]	8	[ ]
9	[ ]	9	[ ]

13. 5 7 10 14 XX 25 32 40

0	[ ]	0	[ ]
1	[ ]	1	[ ]
2	[ ]	2	[ ]
3	[ ]	3	[ ]
4	[ ]	4	[ ]
5	[ ]	5	[ ]
6	[ ]	6	[ ]
7	[ ]	7	[ ]
8	[ ]	8	[ ]
9	[ ]	9	[ ]

14. 23 20 17 XX 11 8 5

0	[ ]	0	[ ]
1	[ ]	1	[ ]
2	[ ]	2	[ ]
3	[ ]	3	[ ]
4	[ ]	4	[ ]
5	[ ]	5	[ ]
6	[ ]	6	[ ]
7	[ ]	7	[ ]
8	[ ]	8	[ ]
9	[ ]	9	[ ]

15. ½ ¼ ¾ 1 ⅞ ˣ¾

0	[	]	0	[	]
1	[	]	1	[	]
2	[	]	2	[	]
3	[	]	3	[	]
4	[	]	4	[	]
5	[	]	5	[	]
6	[	]	6	[	]
7	[	]	7	[	]
8	[	]	8	[	]
9	[	]	9	[	]

16. 121 36 157 193 3XX

0	[	]	0	[	]
1	[	]	1	[	]
2	[	]	2	[	]
3	[	]	3	[	]
4	[	]	4	[	]
5	[	]	5	[	]
6	[	]	6	[	]
7	[	]	7	[	]
8	[	]	8	[	]
9	[	]	9	[	]

17. 100 1 101 102 XX3

0 [ ]	0 [ ]
1 [ ]	1 [ ]
2 [ ]	2 [ ]
3 [ ]	3 [ ]
4 [ ]	4 [ ]
5 [ ]	5 [ ]
6 [ ]	6 [ ]
7 [ ]	7 [ ]
8 [ ]	8 [ ]
9 [ ]	9 [ ]

18. 5 2 10 20 200 XX00

0 [ ]	0 [ ]
1 [ ]	1 [ ]
2 [ ]	2 [ ]
3 [ ]	3 [ ]
4 [ ]	4 [ ]
5 [ ]	5 [ ]
6 [ ]	6 [ ]
7 [ ]	7 [ ]
8 [ ]	8 [ ]
9 [ ]	9 [ ]

19. 12 -24 36 -48 XX

0	[ ]	0	[ ]
1	[ ]	1	[ ]
2	[ ]	2	[ ]
3	[ ]	3	[ ]
4	[ ]	4	[ ]
5	[ ]	5	[ ]
6	[ ]	6	[ ]
7	[ ]	7	[ ]
8	[ ]	8	[ ]
9	[ ]	9	[ ]

20. 42 -33 24 -15 XX

0	[ ]	0	[ ]
1	[ ]	1	[ ]
2	[ ]	2	[ ]
3	[ ]	3	[ ]
4	[ ]	4	[ ]
5	[ ]	5	[ ]
6	[ ]	6	[ ]
7	[ ]	7	[ ]
8	[ ]	8	[ ]
9	[ ]	9	[ ]

21. 12 XX   −8 −6 4 2

0	[ ]	0	[ ]
1	[ ]	1	[ ]
2	[ ]	2	[ ]
3	[ ]	3	[ ]
4	[ ]	4	[ ]
5	[ ]	5	[ ]
6	[ ]	6	[ ]
7	[ ]	7	[ ]
8	[ ]	8	[ ]
9	[ ]	9	[ ]

22. 2 −¼ 6 −⅛ XX

0	[ ]	0	[ ]
1	[ ]	1	[ ]
2	[ ]	2	[ ]
3	[ ]	3	[ ]
4	[ ]	4	[ ]
5	[ ]	5	[ ]
6	[ ]	6	[ ]
7	[ ]	7	[ ]
8	[ ]	8	[ ]
9	[ ]	9	[ ]

23. 1 3 7 15 XX

0	[	]	0	[	]
1	[	]	1	[	]
2	[	]	2	[	]
3	[	]	3	[	]
4	[	]	4	[	]
5	[	]	5	[	]
6	[	]	6	[	]
7	[	]	7	[	]
8	[	]	8	[	]
9	[	]	9	[	]

24. 1 $\frac{1}{3}$ 9 $\frac{1}{27}$ XX

0	[	]	0	[	]
1	[	]	1	[	]
2	[	]	2	[	]
3	[	]	3	[	]
4	[	]	4	[	]
5	[	]	5	[	]
6	[	]	6	[	]
7	[	]	7	[	]
8	[	]	8	[	]
9	[	]	9	[	]

25. 4 5 10 28 82 XX4

0	[	]	0	[	]
1	[	]	1	[	]
2	[	]	2	[	]
3	[	]	3	[	]
4	[	]	4	[	]
5	[	]	5	[	]
6	[	]	6	[	]
7	[	]	7	[	]
8	[	]	8	[	]
9	[	]	9	[	]

26. 123 571 113 17X X23

0	[	]	0	[	]
1	[	]	1	[	]
2	[	]	2	[	]
3	[	]	3	[	]
4	[	]	4	[	]
5	[	]	5	[	]
6	[	]	6	[	]
7	[	]	7	[	]
8	[	]	8	[	]
9	[	]	9	[	]

End of Mock test 2

You will find the answers to this mock test at the end of the
chapter.

Answers to Chapter 3

Part 1

1. 80,000
2. 391 miles
3. £123.30
4. 2,925
5. 49,699
6. 43 units
7. 2,380
8. £16.48
9. 3,600
10. 37
11. 235
12. 10 pence
13. 1⁵⁄₃₆
14. 1⅞
15. 1610
16. 5.66
17. 0.0625
18. 17.87
19. 7:2
20. 500
21. 60 cl
22. 12.25
23. £14.25
24. 84
25. £2.15
26. £27.75
27. £4,255.32
28. $x = \dfrac{1,800}{3} + 1,000$
29. 60%
30. 14
31. 576

Part 3

1.	125	31.	£84
2.	48	32.	£680.85
3.	1600 gallons	33.	£30:£20
4.	£268.80	34.	A = 100 B = 500 C = 400
5.	£35.74	35.	3:10
6.	105,000	36.	15:6:4
7.	5 mph	37.	240
8.	£60,800	38.	£2448
9.	¹⁄₂₀ pound	39.	£37.38
10.	120	40.	£2400
11.	£450	41.	28 mph
12.	£198,000	42.	3½ hours
13.	£16.80	43.	30 minutes
14.	£4.50	44.	£80.19
15.	£2	45.	20 minutes
16.	62%	46.	£22,368
17.	1:49	47.	6,667 votes
18.	16%	48.	23
19.	£315.25	49.	1
20.	28 pence	50.	£15,063.15
21.	£42.50	51.	14
22.	18 inches	52.	528
23.	£13,382.26	53.	504
24.	£200	54.	2
25.	£165.31	55.	1,500
26.	60%	56.	5
27.	£350	57.	128
28.	£10.58	58.	131
29.	£350	59.	243
30.	£85.11	60.	216

Part 4

Mock test 1

1.	C	13.	B
2.	E	14.	C
3.	A	15.	D
4.	E	16.	E
5.	D	17.	A
6.	B	18.	C
7.	E	19.	B
8.	A	20.	F
9.	F	21.	C
10.	D	22.	F
11.	C	23.	A
12.	D		

Mock test 2

1.	59	14.	40
2.	12	15.	11
3.	44	16.	50
4.	99	17.	20
5.	40	18.	40
6.	92	19.	60
7.	62	20.	06
8.	09	21.	10
9.	08	22.	10
10.	10	23.	31
11.	12	24.	81
12.	08	25.	24
13.	19	26.	19

Chapter 4
Relearn the rules of English usage

To write or speak English, or for that matter any natural language, involves rules of usage called grammar.

To speak, or write, correctly you do not need to recite the rules of usage. Grammar classes at school can be a distant, possibly bad, memory and the content of those lessons long forgotten. To speak or write correctly all that is required is that you apply the rules correctly – that you implicitly follow the rules.

In the context of the psychometric test, however, the correct application of the rules is insufficient. To do well in such tests it is necessary that you know, as well as follow, the rules of usage. For most people, this requires a certain amount of revision. It is well worth the effort. The test candidate who knows the rules will be far more confident, will realise what is behind the examiner's questions and will recognise the significance of the subtle differences in the suggested answers.

What follows is a statement of the rules of English relevant to psychometric tests. The practice questions that follow the glossary allow you to practise the rules; the mock tests allow you to practise under test conditions.

Part 1

Glossary

Adjective

An adjective adds detail to a noun or pronoun. To say, for example, that the record was scratched is to add the adjective 'scratched' to the noun 'record'.

Adjectives can also limit or define. For this reason it is proper to think of them as modifiers. For example, if we say that 'Few people enjoy the game' the adjective 'few' limits rather than describes the noun 'people'.

Adverb

An adverb modifies a verb. It can detail, limit or define. If we say, for example, 'The yacht was sinking fast', the adverb 'fast' adds detail to the verb 'sinking'. 'Not' and 'very' are adverbs. An adverb can also add detail to an adjective (very few) or another adverb (very fast).

Note that adjectives and adverbs can be either phrases or words. In this statement 'The people opposite me enjoyed the game', the phrase 'opposite me' limits the noun 'people', so is an adjective.

Apposition

An appositional word or phrase is a noun or pronoun placed next to another noun or pronoun. It has the same meaning but its function is to rename or identify the subject. For example, if I were to say, 'The child, Junior, drank all the milk', I would be introducing a one-word apposition: 'Junior'. An example of an appositional phrase is 'a one-year-old' in the statement 'The child, a one-year-old, drank all the milk'.

Article

Articles modify nouns. They are either indefinite or definite. 'A' and 'an' are indefinite articles because they modify a singular noun which is general. The article 'the' is particular so is used to modify a particular noun.

Clause

A clause is a group of words within a sentence which contains a subject and a verb. If you were to say, for example, 'They bought the camera in order to photograph the baby' you have two clauses: first clause, 'They bought the camera' (subject 'camera', verb 'bought'); second clause, 'in order to photograph the baby' (subject 'baby', verb 'photograph').

There are two types of clause:

Main clause

A main clause expresses a complete thought and makes sense on its own. The example 'They bought the camera' is a main clause.

Subordinate clause

A subordinate clause on its own does not make sense or express a complete thought. 'In order to photograph the baby' is an example of a subordinate clause.

Complement

The basic parts of a sentence are a subject, a verb and a complement. The complement follows the subject and verb to complete the meaning. It can be any word or phrase. For example:

'Scott went on holiday' (The complement is the noun 'holiday', 'Scott' the subject and 'went' the verb.)

'Describe the taste to me.' (The complement is the pronoun 'me', 'taste' the subject, and 'describe' the verb.)

Conjunction

A conjunction is a word which joins words, phrases or clauses. A conjunction can either treat clauses equally or make one more important. A coordinating conjunction connects without making either part more important and usually involves a comma being placed before the conjunction. Examples are 'or', 'for', 'but' and 'nor'. A subordinating conjunction makes the clause it begins less important. Examples are 'as', 'because', 'when' and 'which'.

Direct object

A direct object is a complement to which the verb in a sentence is directed. It is either a noun or pronoun, phrase or clause. In the example provided in the entry for Complement, both the words 'holiday' and 'me' are direct objects of the verbs 'went' and 'describe' respectively.

Gerund

A gerund is used as a noun but is formed from a verb (so it is a verbal; see below). It ends in '-ing' and often begins a phrase. For example:

'Playing all day was exhausting.' (The gerund is 'playing', formed from the verb 'to play', but used in this context as a noun.)

'Smoking causes cancer.'

'She loves cycling in the open countryside.' (In this instance, the gerund is not at the beginning of the sentence.)

Indirect object

A sentence that contains an indirect object must also contain a direct object because the former indicates to whom or what the action of the verb is directed. Like a direct object, an indirect object is a complement. For example, take the sentence 'Thomas wanted the videos for his students'. In this case the subject is 'Thomas', the verb 'wanted', the direct object 'the videos' and the indirect object 'his students'.

Infinitive

An infinitive consists of the word 'to' followed by a verb used as either a noun, an adjective or an adverb. For example: 'To smile is bliss' (the verb 'to smile' is here used as a noun).

'If only you were to smile' (the verb 'to smile' is here being used as an adverb).

Watch out for split infinitives. A split infinitive has an adverb placed between the 'to' and the verb. A famous example is 'to boldly go'. To avoid splitting the infinitive the phrase should read 'to go boldly'.

Modifier

A modifier adds information and may take the form of a word, a phrase or a clause. Adjectives, adverbs and articles are examples of modifiers.

Misplaced modifier

A modifier is misplaced if, in a sentence, it modifies the wrong word; if it seems to describe a thing or person other than the thing or person it should describe. To correct the situation, you simply move the modifier. For example:

'The reporter went to the press briefing to hear about the escaped lion with a tape recorder.'

This should have read:

'The reporter with a tape recorder went to the press briefing to hear about the escaped lion.'

Dangling modifier

A modifier is said to dangle if it cannot be attached to the subject of the main clause, so unless the sentence is changed it has nothing to modify. For example:

'Before writing a press release, the reader should be considered.' The phrase 'Before writing a press release' is a dangling modifier because it does not have a subject to modify. To correct the situation the sentence would have to be changed so that it read, for example:

> 'Before writing a press release, the writer should consider the reader.'

Noun

A noun is a word, a clause or a phrase which identifies a person, a place, an idea or a thing. There are five types of noun:

Proper noun

A proper noun names a particular person, place or thing. Examples of proper nouns are 'Tony', 'Frances' and 'Taj Mahal'. Note that proper nouns always begin with a capital letter.

Common noun

A common noun identifies a general thing, a place or a kind of person. For example: 'house', 'village green' or 'traffic warden'.

Collective noun

Collective nouns are singular but they identify groups of individuals. For example: 'audience', 'class' and 'crowd'.

Concrete noun

Concrete nouns identify inanimate objects such as 'mineral', 'metal', 'paper' and 'feather'. Common nouns can also be concrete nouns; for example, chair and table are both common and concrete nouns.

Abstract noun

Abstract nouns identify qualities and ideals such as 'truth', 'justice' and 'intelligence'.

Participle

A participle is formed from a verb which is used like an adjective. A present participle ends in '-ing' while a past participle usually ends in '-ed', '-en' or '-t'. An example of a present participle is 'paying' in the sentence: 'Paying tax is a necessary evil.' An example of a past participle is 'celebrated' in the sentence: 'The celebrated climber gave a speech.'

Watch out for dangling participial phrases. A participial phrase begins with a participle. It is dangling if there is no noun or pronoun to which it adds detail. For example, the following statement contains a dangling participial phrase:

'Having finished the crossword, the dog went out into the garden.'

The participial phrase 'Having finished the crossword' is dangling because there is no sensible noun or pronoun to which it relates. To make the statement sensible, you would need to provide a noun or pronoun. For example:

'Having finished the crossword, Thomas went out into the garden with the dog.'

Parts of speech

There are eight basic types of word: nouns, pronouns, verbs, adjectives, adverbs, prepositions, conjunctions and interjectives.

Pronoun

A pronoun can be used in place of a noun. For example:

'The water was warm, and it remained so all day.'

The pronoun 'it' has been used in this sentence in place of the noun 'water'.

When replacing nouns with pronouns you must take care that you do not introduce ambiguity. For example: 'The water remained warm all day and it was the warmest I can remember'. In this instance it is unclear whether it is the water or the day that was the warmest in memory. When there is a risk of ambiguity the noun should be repeated. For example, in the above case the ambiguity is removed if we write: 'The water remained warm all day, the warmest day I can remember'.

There are a great many types of pronoun and they are classified by function. The list here is not exhaustive:

Demonstrative pronouns:	This, that, these, those
Interrogative pronouns:	Which, who, whom, what, whose
Personal pronouns:	I, he, you, she, us, them
Possessive pronouns:	My, mine, your, its, his, her, our, their
Indefinite pronouns:	All, both, few, many, some

Sentence

A sentence must have a subject and a verb and express a complete thought. For example, the statement 'Opera began' has a subject (Opera) and a verb (began) but does not express a complete thought, so is not a sentence. The situation is easily corrected if we write, 'The Opera began', as this does express a complete thought and so is a sentence.

'They cried' is an example of a sentence which comprises no more than a subject and a verb yet still expresses a complete thought.

Sentences are classified according to what they express or by their structure. In the context of psychometric tests, their classification according to structure is more relevant.

Sentences can be classified under four types of structure. These are:

1. Simple sentences

A simple sentence comprises one main clause only. So remember that a main clause can be a sentence. Examples are usually short, for instance, 'She hates grammar'; but they need not be, as the following example illustrates:

'The assistant editor made over twenty suggested alterations in the first few pages of text.'

2. Compound sentences

A compound sentence has a multiple of main clauses (two or more). For example:

1st main clause:	'Come and see our range of mountain bikes
Connective	and
2nd main clause	we will be pleased to demonstrate any model.'

3. Complex sentences

A complex sentence comprises one main clause and one or more subordinate clauses. For example:

Subordinate clause	After having a bath
Main clause	Thomas felt a lot better.

4. Compound-complex sentences

These comprise two or more main clauses and one or more subordinate clauses. For example:

1st main clause	Thomas so enjoyed the opera
1st subordinate clause	which he had heard was good
2nd main clause	that he vowed to go each week
2nd subordinate clause	assuming he could obtain tickets.

In English usage tests, look out for two or more sentences which are joined by a comma or have no punctuation separating them, for example: 'The sun shone, they were very happy.' This kind of error is often examined and can be corrected with either a full stop, a semicolon or the use of the conjunction 'and' in place of the comma.

Another commonly tested error involves a phrase or subordinate clause being presented as a sentence.

Subject

A subject is the word or words being talked about in the sentence. A subject is often a noun but can be a pronoun, a verbal noun (but not a participle), a phrase or clause. A subject has one or more verbs which tell what the subject is doing.

The subject is underlined in the following sentences:

'<u>Oystercatchers</u> are black and white wading birds.'
(Subject as a noun)

'After showering, she went to work.'
(Subject as a pronoun)

'<u>Rain making</u> is impossible.'
(Subject as a gerund phrase)

'<u>What is happening</u> is quite the most extraordinary thing imaginable.'
(Subject as a subordinate clause)

Tense

Tense shows the moment to which a verb refers. A simple tense can show the past, present or future. For example: he swam, he swims, he will swim. What are called perfect tenses can be further subdivided (notice that all three contain past participles):

1. Present perfect tense. This shows that an action which began in the past is continuing or has been completed in the present. For example: 'Birthdays are always celebrated.'
2. Past perfect (or pluperfect) tense. This shows that an action was completed before a past point in time. For example: 'Gino had finished his birthday celebration by midnight.'
3. Future perfect tense. This shows that a future action will be completed after another future action. For example: 'By the time this book is published, my first child will have been born.'

In a verbal usage exam, always check that the tenses of a sentence are not mixed up. In particular, ensure that the verb in the subordinate clause has the same tense as the verb in the main clause.

A verb tells what someone, or something, is or does, its state or condition. There are two types of action verb, transitive and intransitive. 'She <u>publishes</u> books': 'publishes' is a transitive verb because it is followed by a direct object. In the sentence, 'The river <u>winds</u> through the hills', 'winds' is an intransitive verb as it is not followed by a direct object. There are also linking verbs; for example, 'The sea <u>looks</u> green' and 'she is accomplished' – these tell us what someone or something is.

Questions in selection tests are sometimes on the characteristics of verbs, in particular the number, person and tense of verb.

1. Number

A verb must agree with the number of its subject. If, for example, the subject is plural, so must the verb be. Consider an example: 'Mother and baby does well' is incorrect because the subject is plural while the verb is singular.

2. Person

A verb can be in the first, second or third person (singular or plural) and serves to establish whether or not the subject is speaking, being addressed or being spoken about. The same verb form often applies to different persons or numbers:

'We <u>won</u> the race.' (plural first person)
'You <u>won</u> the race.' (singular or plural second person)
'They <u>won</u> the race.' (plural third person)

3. Tense

Tense shows whether or not the verb refers to the past, present or future. The verb of any subordinate clause must agree with the tense of the main clause. For example, the sentence 'After he read the paper, Jon asks anyone else if they would like to read it', is incorrect because the verb in the main clause is in the present tense while the verb in the subordinate clause is in the past tense.

Verbal

A verbal is derived from a verb but is not used as such. Verbals are, instead, used as either nouns, adjectives or infinitives. See Gerund, Participle and Infinitive for examples.

Now practise these rules by attempting the questions in Part 2 of this chapter.

Part 2

Practice questions

Identify the *correct* sentences:

1.

A   There are redundancies when the managing director arrived.

B   There will be redundancies after the managing director arrived.

C   After the new managing director arrived, there were redundancies.

D   After the new managing director arrived, there will be many redundancies.

E   None of these.

Answer

2.

A   As soon as the sales figures are available, the directors knew they had achieved their targets.

B   As soon as the sales figures were available, the directors knew they had achieved their targets.

C   As soon as the sales figures are available, the directors knew they have achieved their targets.

D   None of these.

Answer

3.

A   Although the business plan look promising the bank manager suspected that the proposal is unlikely to succeed.

B   Although the business plan looks promising the bank manager suspects the proposal was unlikely to succeed.

C   Although the business plan looked promising the bank manager suspected that the proposal was unlikely to succeed.

D   None of these.

Answer

4.

A   If you were to contact the client you might find that they would buy.

B   If you are to contact the client you might find that they would buy

C   If you were to contact the client you will find that they will buy.

D   None of these.

Answer

5.

A   While the photocopier is broken you will have to go across the road to the copy shop.

B   While the photocopier was broken you will have to go across the road to the copy shop.

C   When the photocopier is broken you went across the road to the copy shop.

D   None of these.

Answer

[ ]

6.

A   My new colleague is the one who has the red car.

B   My new colleague was the one whom had the red car.

C   My new colleague will be the one who had the red car.

D   None of these.

Answer

[ ]

7.

A   The family will eating their meal in the restaurant.

B   The family was eating its meal in the restaurant.

C   The family were eating their meal in the restaurant.

D   None of these.

Answer

[ ]

8.

A   Neither you nor I is able to make sense of this.

B   Neither you nor I are able to make sense of this.

C   Neither you nor I will be able to make sense of this.

D   None of these.

Answer

9.

A   Bill, as well as the rest of his colleagues, is going to the annual office dinner.

B   Bill, as well as the rest of his colleagues, are going to the annual office dinner.

C   Neither of these.

Answer

10.

A   You girls over there what do you think you are doing.

B   You girl over there what do you think you are doing.

C   Neither of these.

Answer

Identify any *incorrect* sentences. The error for which you are looking is a dangling participle phrase.

11.

A Having read of the outbreak of unrest in Africa, Joe heard the next day that war had broke out.

B The Prime Minister decided to recall Parliament; he faced a sea of very grave faces when he rose to make his statement.

C Having read of the outbreak of unrest in Africa, the next day war broke out.

D None of these.

Answer

12.

A Wishing the department to succeed, new staff were taken on.

B It was clear that the Prime Minister had written off the by-election result; he intended to blame it on the recession.

C Neither of these.

Answer

13.

A   After having finished the exam, the candidates felt a great sense of relief.

B   Feeling tired of the run, Hope decided to take a bath.

C   My mother accused me of being mad, talking to myself all the time.

D   None of these.

Answer

14.

A   The mosquitoes drove him mad, walking through the jungle.

B   When we got to the house, having walked for many hours, we simply fell into bed and slept.

C   Neither of these.

Answer

15.

A   Tests play an important role in the allocation of opportunities; their use, therefore, should be closely controlled.

B   Woken from sleep by the bright sunshine, Mary decided to get up straightaway.

C   Beaten roundly in battle by the French army, the English decided to sue for peace.

D   None of these.

Answer

*Split infinitive*s – identify the *incorrect* sentence:

16.

A   From the age of three it was clear that Alison was going to quickly go to the top of the class.

B   From the age of three it was clear that Alison was going to go to quickly to the top of the class.

C   Neither of these.

Answer

17.

A   After going on her training course Susan was skilful in the way she managed to coordinate the concurrent sales and marketing conferences.

B   After going on her training course Susan was able to coordinate skilfully the concurrent sales and marketing conferences.

C   Neither of these.

Answer

18.

A   It was clear that to precipitately press ahead would have been a mistake.

B   It was clear that to press ahead precipitately would have been a mistake.

C   Neither of these.

Answer

19.

A He wanted, at an accelerated pace, to move ahead, but his boss prevented him from doing so.

B He wanted to move ahead at an accelerated pace, but his boss prevented him from doing so.

C Neither of these.

Answer

20.

A The sales team wished to really work hard in order to achieve their targets.

B The sales team wished really to work hard in order to achieve their targets.

C Neither of these.

Answer

21.

A Hoping to make amends, therefore, the Prime Minister called a special meeting of her cabinet.

B Hoping to, therefore, make amends the Prime Minister called a special meeting of his cabinet.

C Neither of these.

Answer

The following sentences test your understanding of the use of *apostrophes*. Identify the *correct* sentences. Note that more than one sentence may be correct.

22.
A   It's a good thing you gave the baby lamb it's extra milk during the night.
B   It's a good thing you gave the baby lamb its extra milk during the night.
C   It is a good thing you gave the baby lamb its extra milk during the night.
D   None of these.

Answer

23.
A   Put the boys' shoes on otherwise their feet will get wet.
B   Put the boy's shoes on otherwise their feet will get wet.
C   Put the boys' shoes on otherwise his feet will get wet.
D   None of these.

Answer

Useful tip:
'Its' (when used as a possessive) is an exception to the rule and does not take an apostrophe.
    Remember – the abbreviated form of 'it is' or 'it has' is 'it's', with an apostrophe.

24.

A   Miles's achievement at cricket will long be remembered at his old school.

B   Miles's achievements at cricket will long be remembered at his old school.

C   Mile's achievement at cricket will long be remembered at his old school.

D   None of these.

Answer

25.

A   The 60s were a time when sexual liberation was first condoned.

B   The 60's were a time when sexual liberation was first condoned.

C   The sixty's were a time when sexual liberation was condoned.

D   None of these.

Answer

26.

A   The forecast for todays weather predicts rain, but tomorrow it's going to be fine.

B   The forecast for today's weather predicts rain, but tomorrow its going to be fine.

C   The forecast for todays weather predicts rain, but tomorrow its going to be fine.

D   None of these

Answer

Some tests require you to decide between *parts of a sentence* and identify which is *correct*.

With the following examples, your task is to identify which of the suggested parts complete the sentence correctly.

27.

Central banks had to step in to prop up the European Exchange Rate Mechanism...

A   tomorrow if massive selling is not to threaten the French franc.

B   yesterday as massive selling threatened the French franc.

C   Neither of these.

Answer

28.

… cash offer under its recently announced enhanced dividend plan have come off best.

A   The shareholders who subscribed to the companys.
B   The shareholder who sub-scribed for the company's.
C   The shareholder who subscribed to the company's.
D   None of these.

Answer

29.

Receivers were called in but they will attempt to keep the company trading…

A   it all depends on whether there are sufficient funds to pay salaries due on the last day of the month.
B   and decide whether the company has sufficient funds to pay the salaries due on the last day of the month.
C   if there are sufficient funds to pay this month's salaries.
D   None of these.

Answer

30.

… they were frequently amended to allow for individual projects to be approved.

A   Policy guidelines, agreed by the committee, however,

B   Policy guidelines were agreed by the committee,

C   Policy guidelines were agreed by the committee; however,

D   None of these.

Answer

31.

… from the opposition when he called on them to change their minds and vote with the government.

A   He elicited a baying increase of support.

B   He elated a tremendous increase in support.

C   He elicited a baying crescendo of support.

D   None of these.

Answer

Use of *negatives*

32.

Only one of the following sentences is *incorrect*; which one is it?

A   'You don't want not to do that, do you?'

B   'I should not bother washing the car, dear,' said a wife to her husband, to which he replied, 'I can't not do it; it looks disgraceful.'

C   He was stopped by the beggar, but hadn't got any money.

D   You should not think there are no examples when killing could be warranted.

E   It's not impossible that we will be able to get away tonight before 7 o'clock.

Answer

Use of *capitals*

33.

The capitalisation of three of the following sentences is *incorrect*. Which sentences are they?

A   A person who comes from France will usually speak French.

B   It was William Shakespeare who first coined the phrase 'all the world's a stage'.

C   The Government buildings have all been renovated.

D   After the management buy-out, Nicholas Smith took over as the new Managing Director.

E   When asked which book he would take on his desert island, he said '*The Catcher in the Rye*'.

F   Every morning we had to swear allegiance to the american flag.

G   The Church situated on the corner is called The Church of St John.

H   Sitting in the conference room were a group of managers, directors and other senior executives.

Answer

34.

Which of the following include *incomplete sentences* or do not form complete sentences?

A   He bought the Australian newspaper group. In order to complete his domination of the world's press.

B   To err is human.

C   'Passing my driving test is my greatest achievement so far'. She said.

D   The exhausted cyclist.

E   She got tanned. And the sun shone at the weekend.

F   Somewhere over the rainbow.

G   Having worked, she now decided to retire.

Answer

Practice punctuation

35. Which of the following sentences is correctly punctuated?

A   For the sales conference, Alison had to check the seating, the lighting, the pen situation and the catering.

B   For the sales conference, Alison had to check the seating, the lighting, the pen situation, and the catering.

C   Neither sentence.

Answer

36.

A   There were four boys chosen for the job; Toby, Scott, Miles and Mark.

B   There were four boys chosen for the job: Toby, Scott, Miles and Mark.

C   Neither sentence.

Answer

37.

A   Although he could not be sure of his map reading, he decided to turn left at the next junction.

B   Although he could not be sure of his map reading he decided to turn left at the next junction.

C   Neither of these.

Answer

38.

A   Yes – he interjected, for he had to say exactly what he felt.

B   Yes; he interjected, for he had to say exactly what he felt.

C   Neither sentence.

Answer

39.

A   Max, Bill and Geoff were in the room. So which boy's hat is this?

B   Max, Bill and Geoff were in the room. So which boys' hat is this?

C   Neither sentence.

Answer

40.

A   The M25 is to be made into a 16-lane highway, many local residents find this unacceptable.

B   The M25 is to made into a 16-lane highway; many local residents find this unacceptable.

C   Neither sentence.

Answer

41.

A   He decided to become a full time student.

B   He decided to become a full-time student.

C   Neither sentence.

Answer

42.

A Would they need to ask the permission of the farmer to cross his land? it wasn't quite clear from the notice.

B Would they need to ask the permission of the farmer to cross his land; it wasn't clear from the notice.

C Neither sentence.

Answer

43.

A The MP, Crispin Biggs-Williams, was the first to declare his anti European intentions by waving his jacket – a brightly striped old Wellington blazer – and was first into the opposition lobby.

B The MP Crispin Biggs-Williams, was the first to declare his anti Europeans intentions by waving his jacket – a brightly striped old Wellington blazer – and was first into the opposition lobby.

C Neither sentence.

Answer

44.

A 'I am enjoying this' – he said, dreamily.

B 'I am enjoying this' – he said, dreamily.

C Neither sentence.

Answer

Useful tips:
When itemising a list do not include a comma before the final 'and' unless there has already been an 'and' in the list and a comma is needed for clarity. For example, had question 35 above read: 'For the sales conference, Alison had to check the seating, the lighting, the pen and paper situation, and the catering' then a comma before the final 'and' would be correct.

Nouns which are linked together to describe another noun and precede it usually take a hyphen. For example, 'air-raid warden'.

Remember – question marks and exclamation marks incorporates full stops and can, therefore, conclude a sentence.

Common spelling mistakes

45.
Underline the *incorrect* spellings below:

1.	accomodation	16.	shelfs
2.	miniscule	17.	shere
3.	the affect	18.	sieve
4.	targetted	19.	bourgeoisy
5.	the business practice	20.	necessarily
6.	fulfill	21.	disatisfaction
7.	the current climate	22.	trully
8.	the stationery car	23.	remittance
9.	the principle's office	24.	nascent
10.	indispensable	25.	reminisence
11.	despairately	26.	conscientous
12.	seperately	27.	nationaly
13.	the mother's dependants	28.	potatoe
14.	abysmaly	29.	liklihood
15.	independent	30.	psycopath

31. surreptitiously
32. participle
33. address
34. yatch
35. rooves
36. noticable
37. unnoticed
38. disoluble
39. realise
40. anti-clockwise

41. proceed
42. preceed
43. munifiscent
44. personel
45. persistant
46. perpetretor
47. jewellery
48. encyclopedia
49. inquiry
50. benefiting

Useful tips:

In most cases the 't's, 'l's and 'r's in the middle of a word are doubled; for example, pitting, fuelling and recurring. However, at the end of a word there is only one 't', 'l' or 'r'; for example, 'spiteful'. There are exceptions and you should learn the most common of these; examples include fulfil, benefited and targeted.

In most cases the prefixes 'dis', 'un', 'in', etc, take only one 's' or 'n' when attached to another word. However, remember that if the suffix already begins with an 's' or 'n', the letters will be doubled; for example, dissatisfaction and unnatural.

46.

Underline the *correct* choice in the following sentences:

A   He was most $\begin{array}{c}\text{complementary}\\\text{complimentary}\end{array}$ about my new painting.

B   The $\begin{array}{c}\text{effect}\\\text{affect}\end{array}$ you had on the children was to excite them.

C   The tolling of the church bell, striking on the hour, every hour, was $\begin{array}{c}\text{continuous}\\\text{continual}\end{array}$.

D   Before disciplinary action is taken, $\begin{array}{c}\text{advise}\\\text{advice}\end{array}$ should be offered to the member of staff.

E   By the time the starting pistol was fired, the runners were $\begin{array}{c}\text{all ready}\\\text{already}\end{array}$ for the race.

F   The birthday cake was divided $\begin{array}{c}\text{among}\\\text{between}\end{array}$ the many guests.

G   Children, put your toys back $\begin{array}{c}\text{into}\\\text{in}\end{array}$ to the toy box.

H   You will find them $\begin{array}{c}\text{either}\\\text{(no word is required)}\end{array}$ in the wardrobe, on the chair or in the chest-of-drawers.

I   After her engagement, she could not help but $\begin{array}{c}\text{flout}\\\text{flaunt}\end{array}$ her diamond ring at every opportunity.

J   For my holiday in Africa, I was reminded to $\begin{array}{c}\text{take}\\\text{bring}\end{array}$ my malaria tablets.

K   That case is quite different $\begin{array}{c}\text{from}\\\text{than}\end{array}$ the previous one we discussed.

L   Booking is not required for families with $\begin{array}{c}\text{fewer}\\\text{less}\end{array}$ than five members.

M   The pub is about half a mile $^{\text{farther}}_{\text{further}}$ down the road.

N   We will be delighted if Tony and $^{\text{you}}_{\text{yourself}}$ join us for lunch.

O   He had been ^{lying} down for many hours before he was able to shake ^{laying} off his headache.

You will find the answers to these practice questions at the end of the chapter.

Part 3

Mock test

Over the page you will find 25 questions. In some of the sentences over the page, one of the underlined words or phrases is incorrect in terms of English usage. None has more than one error. If you find the error, choose the appropriate letter. If you find no error, choose the letter D. Place your answer in the box.

Do not turn the page until you are ready to begin. Allow yourself 15 minutes to attempt the questions. Work as quickly as you can.

1.   A   B

   <u>Of these</u> dresses, I think this is <u>the prettiest</u>. Do you think

                       C   D

   this is the <u>more prettier</u>? <u>No error</u>

   Answer

2.   A   B

   Giving the ice cream to my sister and <u>I</u>, <u>my father</u> then got

    C   D

   <u>into</u> the car. <u>No error</u>

   Answer

3.   A   B

   Of the two dogs <u>that</u> the family <u>owns</u>, the Labrador is the

          C   D

   <u>fatter</u>. <u>No error</u>

   Answer

4.   A   B
   <u>To who</u> should I send this letter? <u>I</u> asked my boss, as I
       C   D
   <u>paused</u> before his desk. <u>No error</u>

         Answer

         ┌─────────────┐
         │   │
         └─────────────┘

5.   A   B   C
   <u>But</u> is it right <u>that</u> these drugs should be <u>proscribed</u>; that is,
                              D
   taken out of circulation? <u>No error</u>

         Answer

         ┌─────────────┐
         │   │
         └─────────────┘

6.   A   B
   If you <u>were to</u> <u>put fewer</u> than five items in the shopping
                    C   D
   basket, you <u>could</u> go through the express check-out. <u>No
   error</u>

         Answer

         ┌─────────────┐
         │   │
         └─────────────┘

7.

                  A   B   C

In comparison <u>with</u> the <u>English</u>, <u>it is always</u> said that the

                                   D

Irish are more poetic. <u>No error</u>

Answer

8.

               A   B

The line <u>managers</u> were advised that they should<u> council</u>

                                C   D

their staff about the impending <u>take-over</u>. <u>No error</u>

Answer

9.

               A

Since I had <u>learnt </u>to love her so much when she was alive,

        B   C   D

I now <u>treasure</u> my <u>mother's-in-law</u> picture. <u>No error</u>

Answer

10.   A   B   C

The <u>1900s</u> <u>were</u> a time when many <u>Spanish-speaking</u> im-

                                      D

migrants arrived in the USA. <u>No error</u>

Answer

11.   A   B

There was scarcely <u>no one</u> in the room <u>to whom</u> I could

 C   D

<u>have</u> entrusted my secret. <u>No error</u>

Answer

12.   A   B

<u>Taking</u> vitamins is a way of <u>insuring</u> long life, according to

            C   D

the <u>current</u> thinking. <u>No error</u>

Answer

13.   A   B

Each of the <u>hotel's</u> 500 rooms <u>were</u> equipped with tele-

                    C   D

visions, baths, <u>kettles and</u> double beds. <u>No error</u>

Answer

14.   A   B

<u>To do this gradually</u> must be the <u>best</u> tactic, as to do other

         C   D

wise would be to <u>jeopardise</u> the project. <u>No error</u>

Answer

15.   A   B

<u>Entering the house just before midnight,</u> <u>the broken glass</u>

            C D

was discovered by my wife and <u>me.</u> <u>No error</u>

Answer

16. A   B

'How many <u>gin and tonics</u> would you be able to drink in an

     C   D

evening?' <u>He</u> asked. <u>No error</u>

Answer

17.
                                            A

Morphine and other <u>potentially</u> addictive drugs are val-
                       B   C

uable <u>medically;</u> if abused, however, <u>it</u> can cause untold
                        D

damage. <u>No error</u>

                           Answer

18.
                                                  A

According to the village gossip, the <u>local Vicar</u> had <u>to be</u>
      B   C   D

<u>removed</u> from his post for <u>misappropriating</u> funds. <u>No
error</u>

                           Answer

19.
                                    A   B

We've tried to <u>deliberately stop arguing</u> in front of the
                                             C   D

children because we have <u>realised</u> it disturbs them. <u>No
error</u>

                           Answer

20.
                                                  A   B

The following people could be said <u>to have been</u> <u>success-</u>
                C

<u>ful</u> leaders<u>:</u> Margaret Thatcher, Churchill and Charles de
                         D

Gaulle. <u>No error</u>

Answer

21.
          A   B

The <u>children's</u> toys were still <u>laying</u> out on the table when
                         C   D

the parents <u>returned</u>. <u>No error</u>

Answer

22.
                A   B

<u>Paula already left</u> by the time <u>I arrived</u> so I realised that
                                   C

neither she nor I <u>was</u> going to get to the meeting in time.
            D

<u>No error</u>

Answer

23.
                                     A   B

Every man, woman or child on the ship <u>is</u> able to fit <u>into</u>
                                                    C

the lifeboat, so no one should fear for <u>his or her</u> life.
       D

<u>No error</u>

Answer

24.   A   B   C

<u>Which</u> of these two houses belongs to <u>you</u>? <u>Ours</u> is the
                     D

house on the left. <u>No error</u>

Answer

25. A   B

<u>Us</u> women feel that we have suffered <u>too</u> much at the
    C   D

<u>hands</u> of men. <u>No error</u>

Answer

Answers to Chapter 4

Part 2

Correct sentences (page 96)

1.	=	C
2.	=	B
3.	=	C
4.	=	A
5.	=	A
6.	=	A

7. = B Note that family is a collective noun and should therefore take a singular verb.

8. = B
9. = A
10. = C

Incorrect sentences (page 100)

11.	=	C		14.	=	A
12.	=	A		15.	=	D
13.	=	C				

Split infinitives (page 102)

16.	=	A		19.	=	C
17.	=	C		20.	=	A
18.	=	A		21.	=	B

Apostrophes (page 105)

22. = B, C
23. = A
24. = A, B
25. = A. Note that while 60's is often seen in print, this is not correct.
26. = D

Parts of a sentences (page 107)

27. = B
28. = D
29. = C
30. = C
31. = C

Use of negatives (page 110)

32. = A

Use of capitals (page 111)

33. = B, F, G

Incomplete sentences (page 112)

34. = A, C, D, E, F

Practice punctuation (page 112)

35. = A	40. = B	
36. = B	41. = B	
37. = A	42. = C	
38. = C	43. = C	
39. = A	44. = C	

Common spelling mistakes (page 116)

45. You should have underlined numbers:

1, 2, 3, 4, 6 (this is US spelling), 8, 9, 11, 12, 14, 16, 17, 19, 21, 22, 25, 26, 27, 28, 29, 30, 34, 35, 36, 38, 40 (no hyphen), 42, 43, 44, 45

Choice of words (page 118)

46. You should have the following words:

A	=	complimentary	I	=	flaunt
B	=	effect	J	=	take
C	=	continual	K	=	from
D	=	advice	L	=	fewer
E	=	all ready	M	=	farther
F	=	among	N	=	lying
G	=	into			
H	=	no word is required			

Part 3

Mock test

1.	=	C	10.	=	D	19.	=	A
2.	=	A	11.	=	A	20.	=	D
3.	=	A	12.	=	B	21.	=	B
4.	=	A	13.	=	B	22.	=	A
5.	=	A	14.	=	D	23.	=	D
6.	=	D	15.	=	A	24.	=	D
7.	=	D	16.	=	C	25.	=	A
8.	=	B	17.	=	C			
9.	=	C	18.	=	A			

Chapter 5

Lots more really relevant practice

Following procedures

Following procedures measures your ability to follow explicit rules and interpret given information.

Allow yourself 9 minutes to attempt the following 10 questions. You are presented with a choice of 10 possible answers from which you must indicate the correct one(s). Please note that some of the practice questions require more than one suggested answer to be marked as correct.

A credit management process

The flow chart below illustrates the key points of the process.

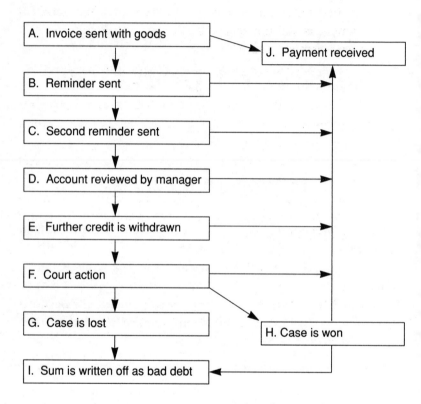

Rules governing the credit process

1. Invoices are sent out with goods and state that the company operates a strict 20-day credit facility from the date of invoice.
2. The first reminder is sent out 14 days after the goods. If payment is still not received, the second reminder is sent after a further 10 days.
3. Account reviews are held 17 days after the issuing of the second reminder.
4. In cases when the sum owed exceeds £100 and payment is not received within 20 days from the date of the account review, court action is instigated.
5. If the court case is lost, the amount is written off as a bad debt.
6. Without exception, credit facilities are withdrawn when the court action is initiated or when any sum becomes more than 60 days overdue.

Questions

1. Payment was received 22 working days after the date of invoice. What stage of the credit process would have last been implemented?

   A   B   C   D   E   F   G   H   I   J
   ☐   ☐   ☐   ☐   ☐   ☐   ☐   ☐   ☐   ☐

2. Court action has had to be initiated against a creditor. What would have been the action taken immediately prior to this?

   A   B   C   D   E   F   G   H   I   J
   ☐   ☐   ☐   ☐   ☐   ☐   ☐   ☐   ☐   ☐

3. A creditor has owed £98 for almost two months. What action should be taken?

   A   B   C   D   E   F   G   H   I   J
   □   □   □   □   □   □   □   □   □   □

4. The average time taken for payment to be received is 39 working days from the invoice date. What stage of the process would next be initiated if payment was not received by then?

   A   B   C   D   E   F   G   H   I   J
   □   □   □   □   □   □   □   □   □   □

5. Identify which stages could precede a debt being written off as bad.

   A   B   C   D   E   F   G   H   I   J
   □   □   □   □   □   □   □   □   □   □

6. A payment has still not been received after 30 days. What action could be taken?

   A   B   C   D   E   F   G   H   I   J
   □   □   □   □   □   □   □   □   □   □

7. What are the possible outcomes from court action?

   A   B   C   D   E   F   G   H   I   J
   □   □   □   □   □   □   □   □   □   □

8. 20 days have passed since a case review. The sum outstanding is £120. What action should be taken?

A	B	C	D	E	F	G	H	I	J
☐	☐	☐	☐	☐	☐	☐	☐	☐	☐

9. What actions can an account manager recommend?

A	B	C	D	E	F	G	H	I	J
☐	☐	☐	☐	☐	☐	☐	☐	☐	☐

10. Since the date of the invoice 41 days have passed. What action is due to be taken?

A	B	C	D	E	F	G	H	I	J
☐	☐	☐	☐	☐	☐	☐	☐	☐	☐

Speed and accuracy

The following speed and accuracy test requires you to compare sets of numbers or letters arranged in pairs, one on the left, the other on the right. Each question comprises four pairs and you have to indicate how many of them are identical. You are offered five possible answers: all four (are identical), three pairs, two pairs, one pair or none.

1. 45981   45981
   xsbaa   xssa
   kiyhq   kiyhq
   21213   21213

All 4	3 pairs	2 pairs	1 pair	None
☐	☐	☐	☐	☐

2. qwdfk   wqdfk
   33601   33611
   15380   15580
   50179   97150

All 4	3 pairs	2 pairs	1 pair	None

3. hjwep   hjwep
   ffthm   ftthm
   abelo   abelo
   mwwgr   mnwgr

All 4	3 pairs	2 pairs	1 pair	None

4. 58392   53892
   dmhmi   dmdmi
   bdbdv   dbdbv
   illia   ilila

All 4	3 pairs	2 pairs	1 pair	None

5. zxasw   zxasw
   74893   74893
   17204   12704
   01010   01020

All 4	3 pairs	2 pairs	1 pair	None

6. bgdth   gbdth
   zakiv   zakii
   45000   54001
   45001   45000

All 4	3 pairs	2 pairs	1 pair	None
☐	☐	☐	☐	☐

7. sopme   soome
   soppq   soppq
   04517   04518
   49872   49872

All 4	3 pairs	2 pairs	1 pair	None
☐	☐	☐	☐	☐

8. mmhhi   mmhhh
   99933   33399
   fffrr   ffrr
   nhqir   nhqir

All 4	3 pairs	2 pairs	1 pair	None
☐	☐	☐	☐	☐

9. nxruy   nxruy
   qqasw   qqasw
   93462   93462
   ntyue   nteyu

All 4	3 pairs	2 pairs	1 pair	None
☐	☐	☐	☐	☐

10. 15795   15795
     48957   48957
     25846   25864
     35745   35754

All 4	3 pairs	2 pairs	1 pair	None

11. ilop   kliop
     kopli   kploi
     poilk   polik
     oolip   ollip

All 4	3 pairs	2 pairs	1 pair	None

12. vfrtg   fgtrv
     gfrtv   gfrtv
     frtgv   frtgv
     gfrtf   rtfgt

All 4	3 pairs	2 pairs	1 pair	None

13. 20250   25052
     0425   0425
     65658   65658
     20052   20052

All 4	3 pairs	2 pairs	1 pair	None

14. blgos   blgos
     werqw   werqw
     14584   14584
     36526   36526

All 4	3 pairs	2 pairs	1 pair	None

15. 07078   07078
     asdfg   asdfg
     gfdsa   gfdsa
     03256   03256

All 4	3 pairs	2 pairs	1 pair	None

16. wuyoi   wuyoi
     30057   30057
     dflkk   dflkk
     45008   45008

All 4	3 pairs	2 pairs	1 pair	None

17. 49057   49057
     00558   00558
     asiore   asoire
     nheppo   nheppo

All 4	3 pairs	2 pairs	1 pair	None

18. 4584584   4584584
    32658   32658
    500505   500505
    054585   0548458

    All 4   3 pairs   2 pairs   1 pair   None
    ☐   ☐   ☐   ☐   ☐

19. gpr ty   gprty
    druowff   druuowff
    foluaw   foluaw
    brtrt   brtrt

    All 4   3 pairs   2 pairs   1 pair   None
    ☐   ☐   ☐   ☐   ☐

20. 137946   137946
    438679   438679
    402794   4022794
    4586003   4586603

    All 4   3 pairs   2 pairs   1 pair   None
    ☐   ☐   ☐   ☐   ☐

21. df er ty s   df er ty s
    fgtyoui   fgtyuoi
    cdf gtyg   cdfgtyy
    mmyyeeq   mmyyyeq

    All 4   3 pairs   2 pairs   1 pair   None
    ☐   ☐   ☐   ☐   ☐

22. fdfre gt   fdre gg
    25 87 5   25 87 5
    bru ew   bru ee
    1579 587   1597 587

All 4	3 pairs	2 pairs	1 pair	None

23. kuyjkrr   kuyjkrr
    qwqwreee qwqwreeee
    nwkyiunn nmkyiunn
    vetuyooi vetyuooi

All 4	3 pairs	2 pairs	1 pair	None

These questions are very easy to make up. If you feel you need more practice, why not create more yourself?

Composite test

You are required to read a passage and, using the information that it contains, decide if the statements listed are true or false.

Each question consists of two statements labelled A and B. This means that there are four possible answers to the questions, namely: both statements are true, both are false, statement A is true, while B is false or B is true while A is false. Your task is to establish which of these situations applies and mark the appropriate box.

Try the following questions. It helps to read the statements before you read the passage.

Passage 1

Mrs Brewer, the office manager, was charged with responsibility for replacing the existing photocopier. The specifications were to remain the same in that the machine was to be able to make 50,000 copies a month, operate at least at 40 copies a minute, have the facility for double-sided copying, a feed tray and a sorter bin. She was told that she could consider ex-demonstration or new machines but must not purchase a service agreement.

Mrs Brewer embarked on the task with some apprehension as she was well aware of the bad reputation of photocopier sales staff. She decided to write out a list of specifications and sent this to a number of companies requesting written quotations and details of their products. Soon afterwards, she started to receive calls from the company representatives offering her all kinds of deals.

Questions

1. Statement: A   Mrs Brewer requested that the sales representatives telephone her.

           B   She wanted a machine which could handle double-sided copying.

A Correct	A Correct	A Incorrect	A Incorrect
B Correct	B Incorrect	B Correct	B Incorrect
☐	☐	☐	☐

2. Statement: A   A service agreement was to be part of the deal.

              B   More features were required of the new machine.

A Correct	A Correct	A Incorrect	A Incorrect
B Correct	B Incorrect	B Correct	B Incorrect
☐	☐	☐	☐

3. Statement: A   Mrs Brewer requires the sales representatives to send her two types of information.

              B   She has a preference for a new machine rather than one that has been reconditioned.

A Correct	A Correct	A Incorrect	A Incorrect
B Correct	B Incorrect	B Correct	B Incorrect
☐	☐	☐	☐

4. Statement: A   While she was apprehensive, Mrs Brewer was able to take some consolation from the fact that she was not solely responsible for the decision over which copier to purchase.

              B   Photocopier sales staff have a reputation.

A Correct	A Correct	A Incorrect	A Incorrect
B Correct	B Incorrect	B Correct	B Incorrect
☐	☐	☐	☐

5. Statement: A Mrs Brewers's copier would need to under-take over half a million copies a year.

              B A machine which could undertake just under 2,000 copies an hour would not meet her specification.

A Correct	A Correct	A Incorrect	A Incorrect
B Correct	B Incorrect	B Correct	B Incorrect
☐	☐	☐	☐

Passage 2

Mr Waters, a tool-maker with Johnson and Matthew, left his machine to record in the company's accident book the fact that he had received a small splinter of steel in his thumb. This was a common accident for someone in his trade and he knew the company nurse would have to remove it, otherwise it was likely to become infected.

As he wrote down the circumstances of his accident he noticed a leaflet which read: 'The Health and Safety at Work Act is aimed at securing the health, safety and welfare of all workers. It requires employers to ensure the safety of their employees at work but also places a legal responsibility on every individual, whilst at work, to take care of their own and their colleagues' health and safety. Workers must cooperate with their employers to ensure that their place of work is safe. The Act allows that both employers and employees can be fined or sent to prison if they fail to fulfil their legal duties. In large organisations health and safety representatives are elected to represent the workers and to carry out safety checks.'

Questions

6. Statement: A   The Act requires every individual to take care to avoid injury to themselves.

             B   Mr Waters has a legal duty to consider the safety of his fellow workers.

A Correct	A Correct	A Incorrect	A Incorrect
B Correct	B Incorrect	B Correct	B Incorrect
☐	☐	☐	☐

7. Statement: A   The Act requires all employers to have safety representatives.

             B   Mr Waters read that he would receive compensation for his injury.

A Correct	A Correct	A Incorrect	A Incorrect
B Correct	B Incorrect	B Correct	B Incorrect
☐	☐	☐	☐

8. Statement: A   Mr Waters' employers risk imprisonment or a fine if they do not maintain a safe place of work.

             B   Mr Waters' thumb required medical attention.

A Correct	A Correct	A Incorrect	A Incorrect
B Correct	B Incorrect	B Correct	B Incorrect
☐	☐	☐	☐

9. Statement: A   Mr Waters is required to record the circumstances of the accident in the accident book.

             B   Fortunately, the book was kept beside Mr Waters' machine.

A Correct	A Correct	A Incorrect	A Incorrect
B Correct	B Incorrect	B Correct	B Incorrect
☐	☐	☐	☐

10. Statement: A   The company provided a written explanation of the Health and Safety at Work Act.

            B   Splinters of metal were an occupational hazard for tool-makers.

A Correct	A Correct	A Incorrect	A Incorrect
B Correct	B Incorrect	B Correct	B Incorrect
☐	☐	☐	☐

Sentence sequence

Below are questions which require you to reorganise four sentences into the order in which they were originally written.

Example:

1. As he moved towards the stove he picked up the oven glove.

2. He took care to make sure that the steam would not scald him and he turned off the gas.

3. James looked up from the paper to notice that the kettle was boiling furiously.

4. He poured the water into the teapot successfully.

```
1 [ ]   1 [ ]   1 [ ]   1 [ ]
2 [ ]   2 [ ]   2 [ ]   2 [ ]
3 [ ]   3 [ ]   3 [ ]   3 [ ]
4 [ ]   4 [ ]   4 [ ]   4 [ ]
```

Correct order 3, 1, 2, 4.

Try these:

1. 1. Put out your arm when you see the bus coming.

   2. Tender the correct change to the conductor.

   3. Climb in.

   4. Tell the conductor where you want to alight.

```
1 [ ]   1 [ ]   1 [ ]   1 [ ]
2 [ ]   2 [ ]   2 [ ]   2 [ ]
3 [ ]   3 [ ]   3 [ ]   3 [ ]
4 [ ]   4 [ ]   4 [ ]   4 [ ]
```

2. 1. The engine roared into life.
    2. The '57 Chevy careered dangerously into the sunset.
    3. There was a stomach-churning grating of the gears.
    4. The tyres squealed as it pulled away.

```
1 [ ]  1 [ ]  1 [ ]  1 [ ]
2 [ ]  2 [ ]  2 [ ]  2 [ ]
3 [ ]  3 [ ]  3 [ ]  3 [ ]
4 [ ]  4 [ ]  4 [ ]  4 [ ]
```

3. 1. The mediaeval period saw a large growth in the construction of cathedrals.
    2. Its main characteristic was parallel stone mullions running the entire height of the windows.
    3. One such was perpendicular Gothic.
    4. They were built in a number of styles.

```
1 [ ]  1 [ ]  1 [ ]  1 [ ]
2 [ ]  2 [ ]  2 [ ]  2 [ ]
3 [ ]  3 [ ]  3 [ ]  3 [ ]
4 [ ]  4 [ ]  4 [ ]  4 [ ]
```

4. 1. The carrots cascaded from the scale pan into the bag.
    2. The grocer deftly spun it before handing it over.
    3. He pulled a paper bag from the hook.
    4. Mr Benjamin placed it into his shopping bag.

```
1 [ ]  1 [ ]  1 [ ]  1 [ ]
2 [ ]  2 [ ]  2 [ ]  2 [ ]
3 [ ]  3 [ ]  3 [ ]  3 [ ]
4 [ ]  4 [ ]  4 [ ]  4 [ ]
```

5. 1. He proffered a flaring match.
   2. 'Have you got a light?' came a once-familiar voice.
   3. In its flickering light he recognised her as his former boss.
   4. He tentatively asked 'Is your name Karen Moss?'

```
1 [ ]   1 [ ]   1 [ ]   1 [ ]
2 [ ]   2 [ ]   2 [ ]   2 [ ]
3 [ ]   3 [ ]   3 [ ]   3 [ ]
4 [ ]   4 [ ]   4 [ ]   4 [ ]
```

6. 1. The former did not reach the South Pole first, but died heroically on his return journey.
   2. There were two Antarctic expeditions in 1912.
   3. The latter, a Norwegian, was the first man to reach the South Pole, but in comparatively unremarkable circumstances.
   4. Arguably, Captain Scott's was more famous than Amundsen's.

```
1 [ ]   1 [ ]   1 [ ]   1 [ ]
2 [ ]   2 [ ]   2 [ ]   2 [ ]
3 [ ]   3 [ ]   3 [ ]   3 [ ]
4 [ ]   4 [ ]   4 [ ]   4 [ ]
```

7. 1. Having bought the shares the stockbroker transferred them to the client.
   2. Before the Big Bang in 1986 the method of buying shares in the London market was different.
   3. The broker then approached a jobber to buy the shares.
   4. The client would approach a stockbroker.

```
1 [ ]  1 [ ]  1 [ ]  1 [ ]
2 [ ]  2 [ ]  2 [ ]  2 [ ]
3 [ ]  3 [ ]  3 [ ]  3 [ ]
4 [ ]  4 [ ]  4 [ ]  4 [ ]
```

8. 1. It is so called because being large, slow and buoyant when dead it was the 'right' whale to catch.
   2. The decline has been the most pronounced among the larger whales, and scientists fear that a number of species, particularly the right whale, might become extinct.
   3. In the 20th century, as fishing methods became more effective, the decline in the whale population occurred very rapidly.
   4. Whales are now protected and their numbers are expected to rise.

```
1 [ ]  1 [ ]  1 [ ]  1 [ ]
2 [ ]  2 [ ]  2 [ ]  2 [ ]
3 [ ]  3 [ ]  3 [ ]  3 [ ]
4 [ ]  4 [ ]  4 [ ]  4 [ ]
```

9. 1. Frantically he tore at the coils around the neck.
   2. Once the bedding was straight, she assured him, 'It's all right, the Doctor's on his way.'
   3. Gently his mother unravelled the sheet and kissed his fevered brow.
   4. The anaconda coiled itself around his body, squeezing the lifeblood from him.

```
1 [ ]   1 [ ]   1 [ ]   1 [ ]
2 [ ]   2 [ ]   2 [ ]   2 [ ]
3 [ ]   3 [ ]   3 [ ]   3 [ ]
4 [ ]   4 [ ]   4 [ ]   4 [ ]
```

10. 1. The Institute claims to show that executive pay in the 1980s outstripped that on the factory floor.
    2. that Britain's executives are threatening the rate of economic recovery by awarding themselves unwarranted pay rises.
    3. The National Institute of Economic and Social Research has apparently confirmed what many have long suspected:
    4. What is more the study found that executive pay rises in the 1990s have little or no connection with company performance.

```
1 [ ]   1 [ ]   1 [ ]   1 [ ]
2 [ ]   2 [ ]   2 [ ]   2 [ ]
3 [ ]   3 [ ]   3 [ ]   3 [ ]
4 [ ]   4 [ ]   4 [ ]   4 [ ]
```

11. 1. After the war he served on the cruiser *Jamaica* in the West Indies.
    2. The son of the naval engineer, Hugo Janier went to Dartmouth at the age of 13 in 1937.
    3. His final post as a captain was in command of the guided-missile destroyer *Bristol*.
    4. Graduating during the war, he saw service as a midshipman on the battleship *Rodney*.

```
1 [ ]   1 [ ]   1 [ ]   1 [ ]
2 [ ]   2 [ ]   2 [ ]   2 [ ]
3 [ ]   3 [ ]   3 [ ]   3 [ ]
4 [ ]   4 [ ]   4 [ ]   4 [ ]
```

12. 1. Having been taken to the police station under arrest, as soon as practicable a decision will be made on whether to press charges.
    2. In the Magistrates Court the case will either be disposed of or adjourned to another sitting.
    3. The suspect should be legally arrested by a police officer, designated official or citizen.
    4. If charged, the suspect will be detained or released on bail to attend the Magistrates Court at a given time on a given day.

```
1 [ ]   1 [ ]   1 [ ]   1 [ ]
2 [ ]   2 [ ]   2 [ ]   2 [ ]
3 [ ]   3 [ ]   3 [ ]   3 [ ]
4 [ ]   4 [ ]   4 [ ]   4 [ ]
```

13. 1. Alternatively, on the verdict of guilty, the defendant will be sentenced immediately or have the case adjourned for sentence in order to allow a pre-sentence report to be made.

    2. At the end of the speeches the judge will sum up the case for the jury, who will then retire in the custody of the jury bailiff to make their deliberations.

    3. Counsel for defence will make her closing speech.

    4. Having given their verdict, the defendant, if she is acquitted, is then free to leave.

```
1 [ ]  1 [ ]  1 [ ]  1 [ ]
2 [ ]  2 [ ]  2 [ ]  2 [ ]
3 [ ]  3 [ ]  3 [ ]  3 [ ]
4 [ ]  4 [ ]  4 [ ]  4 [ ]
```

14. 1. The disaster was narrowly avoided and the track man received a medal and a reward for his bravery.

    2. Imperceptibly at first, the train began to roll down the track, picking up speed.

    3. In his eagerness to get clearance from the signalman the train driver climbed down from the cab, forgetting to apply the brakes.

    4. Seeing another train on the tracks and the impending disaster, the track worker threw down his shovel, leapt into the cab and applied the brake.

```
1 [ ]  1 [ ]  1 [ ]  1 [ ]
2 [ ]  2 [ ]  2 [ ]  2 [ ]
3 [ ]  3 [ ]  3 [ ]  3 [ ]
4 [ ]  4 [ ]  4 [ ]  4 [ ]
```

Data interpretation

This type of question provides numerical data with between two and four questions relating to it which you must answer. It may pay to look at the suggested answers prior to attempting lengthy calculations as it is sometimes possible to rule some of them out and to estimate the correct answer by rounding up sums to more convenient figures. If you do not have sufficient time to finish, try an educated guess. Each suggested answer is given a number. To record your answer you simply mark the answer in the answer box.

Practice questions

Table 1

The table below indicates the total number of young people and what they did after leaving school in the rural districts of an English county between the years 1988 and 1991.

Year	1988	1989	1990	1991
No of school leavers	3,000	2,196	2,400	1,652
Returned to education	450	769	480	798
Entered employment	300	285	240	189
Entered training	600	483	480	266
Unemployed	750	373	480	147
Left district	150	66	120	189
Unknown	750	220	600	63

1. Between the years 1988 and 1990, which after-school activity saw the greatest percentage increase?
    1) returned to education 2) entered training 3) became unemployed 4) left district

1	2	3	4
[ ]	[ ]	[ ]	[ ]

2. How many activities were selected by the same percentage of young people in 1988 and 1990?
    1) two categories 2) four categories 3) five categories 4) three categories

1	2	3	4
[ ]	[ ]	[ ]	[ ]

3. How many more times popular was returning to education compared with entering training in 1991?
    1) five times 2) six times 3) four times 4) three times

1	2	3	4
[ ]	[ ]	[ ]	[ ]

4. Over the four-year period, what was the average number of annual school leavers?
    1) 2,309 2) 3,216 3) 2,312 4) 2,038

1	2	3	4
[ ]	[ ]	[ ]	[ ]

Table 2

The table below illustrates the population structures of countries. The data relate to January 1990.

Country	Total population (millions)	Live births per 1,000	Deaths per 1,000
Country A	56.4	13.2	11.9
Country B	53.6	12.9	12.3
Country C	70.3	11.7	11.6
Country D	12.7	9.9	10.1
Country E	18.2	10.8	11.2

5. Which country is experiencing the fastest rate of growth in population?

   1) A 2) B 3) C 4) E

1	2	3	4
[ ]	[ ]	[ ]	[ ]

6. Which country's population is over four times smaller than country B's?

   1) A 2) B 3) C 4) D

1	2	3	4
[ ]	[ ]	[ ]	[ ]

7. Which country experienced just over 125,000 births?

    1) B 2) C 3) D 4) E

1	2	3	4
[ ]	[ ]	[ ]	[ ]

8. Which two countries experienced a mean rate of death per thousand of 1155?

    1) A and B 2) A and E 3) A and C 4) D and E

1	2	3	4
[ ]	[ ]	[ ]	[ ]

Table 3

The table below shows the monthly average rainfall, hours of sunshine and wind speed for a European country. Consult it to answer the questions below.

	Rainfall (mm)	Sunshine (hours)	Wind speed (knots)
January	91	54	21
February	108	80	17
March	155	140	15
April	160	153	13
May	121	165	12
June	97	228	9
July	78	218	10
August	80	200	11
September	113	193	12
October	102	120	15
November	114	90	16
December	103	64	18

9. What is the mean wind speed for the months of January, February and March?

   1) 18.11 2) 16.66 3) 17.66 4) 15.33

1	2	3	4
[ ]	[ ]	[ ]	[ ]

10. Which three consecutive months have a total of 403 hours of sunshine?

    1) May, June, July 2) October, November, December
    3) March, April, May 4) September, October, November

1	2	3	4
[ ]	[ ]	[ ]	[ ]

11. Identify the percentage which expresses the increase in sunshine between the months of February and March.

    1) 75% 2) 8% 3) 16% 4) 50%

1	2	3	4
[ ]	[ ]	[ ]	[ ]

12. What is the ratio between the rainfall during the wettest and driest months?

    1) 2:1 2) 1:2 3) 1:3 4) 3:1

1	2	3	4
[ ]	[ ]	[ ]	[ ]

Word link

These questions comprise two lines of words, one above the other. On the top line are two words, while on the lower line there are six. Your task is to identify two words in the lower line, one in each half, which forms an analogy when paired with the word in the upper line. You indicate your answer by underlining the two words on the lower line. Although an analogy is when the words are in some way similar, note that in some questions the connection between the words is that they are opposites.

Example questions

1. FLAT   ROUGH
   <u>even</u> taxidermist hatchback   mouse house <u>rugged</u>

The connection in this case is that the words are opposites.

2. FAST   FEAST
   conversion rapid <u>diet</u>   <u>slow</u> gluttony waterfall

The connection is that the opposite of 'fast' is 'slow' and the opposite of 'feast' is 'diet', but note how the connections are made diagonally across the top and bottom line.

3. HORSE   CAR
   putter <u>rider</u> jump   pig <u>driver</u> cow

The connection in this example is that a horse has a rider and a car has a driver.

Practice questions

1. CRICKET
   golf locust vampire

   BAT
   grasshopper club grass

2. SAILOR
   hornpipe ship trumpet

   SURGEON
   xylophone hospital waltz

3. RUN
   sprint manage trot

   CONTROL
   walk regulate relax

4. HIGH
   intoxicate top above

   LOW
   buttock bottom beyond

5. CLOWN
   idiot king approximate

   CIRCUS
   roundabout palace pin

6. ASSEMBLE
   enjoy construct retreat

   WITHDRAW
   age retire superannuate

7. JUDGE
   date court horse

   JOCKEY
   bench club isotherm

8. CONCUR
   agree reject explain

   ARGUE
   propose dispute believe

9. KING
   kong emperor size

   KINGDOM
   empire penguin hall

10. RABBIT
    hearse horse hoarse

    FUR
    hair hare heir

11. YACHT
    care car dinghy

    SAIL
    truck engine outboard

12. DAWN
    patrol stars light

    SUNSET
    moon boulevard dark

13. GOVERNMENT   CHAOS
    free anarchy conservative   liberal order command

14. SOCIALIST   ENVIRONMENTALIST
    red blue black   yellow white green

15. CHINA   FRANCE
    clay tea Asia   polish wine Europe

16. INEPT   PERFECT
    complete apt competent   whole exodus defective

17. DRAWS   ASSESSES
    sketches sledge attractions   praises amalgamate
         appraises

Word swop

Underline the two words which must be interchanged to make the following sentences read sensibly. Do not attempt to alter the sentences in any other way.

1. The Health and Safety at Work Act 1976 is securing at aimed your health, safety and welfare.

2. Unlike most typewritters, when you come to end of a press on a word processor you do not have to line the return key as the word processor brings the cursor to the next line automatically.

3. The equal who gets this job will have a firm commitment to person opportunities.

4. We are housing a London working in north and west association.

5. Holidays grade from 22 to 30 working days annually according to range and length of service.

6. Joyce fell kicking into the chair by the phone, back off her working boots, and went to sleep.

7. Nouns are things words and can name people, creatures, naming and feelings.

8. A subject is a group of sentences which all deal with a single paragraph.

9. In a vault near Paris is kept a small platinum cylinder which serves as the original reference for kilogram standards; copies are sold and made to laboratories worldwide.

10. National Health Service Hospital private have contracts under which they are allowed to top up their pay to a limit of 10% with extra earnings from consultants practice.

11. In his conference speech the Prime Minister worried to provide nursery places for every four-year-old; however, privately, the Education Secretary was pledged because her department had estimated each would cost in the region of £1,500 per annum.

12. The National Heritage Secretary began his speech by saying that, 'There are at present about 30,000 listed buildings of which slightly under 500,000 are grade 1'.

13. Peter Taylor made a virtue of being impressive and his promotion to Chief Executive within three years of joining the company was widely expected but no less predictable.

14. The 24-year-old grandfather whose lord won a Victoria Cross in the First World War appealed to his fellow peers 'not to let our heads rule our hearts'.

15. Imperial porphyry is an exceptionally ancient stone with royal associations from the hard world because pharoahs and emperors chose it for the material from which to build their tombs.

Dominoes

You will be pleased to know that the test does not involve your having to be able to play the real game of dominoes but simply to recognise patterns and determine how many dots there should be in each half of the incomplete domino. Note that in some instances the tests require you to work the numbers 0–6 in a loop, ie 0, 1, 2, 3, 4, 5, 6, 0, 1. Each of the following practice questions has only one answer.

Practical exercises

1.

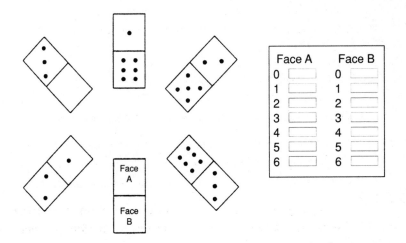

2.

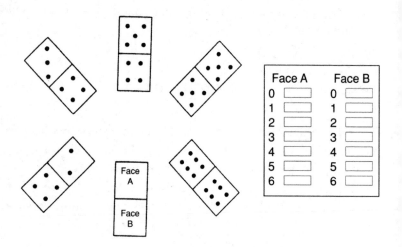

3.

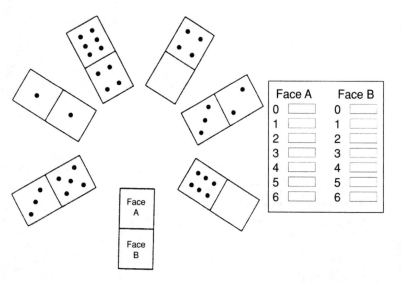

4.

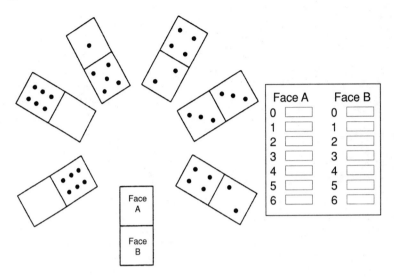

5.

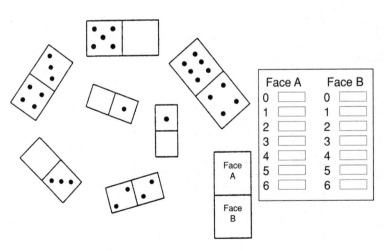

6.

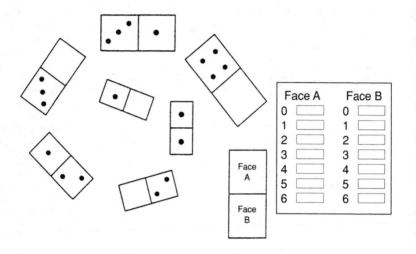

7.

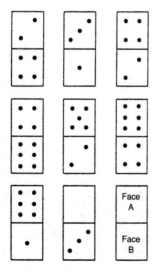

8.

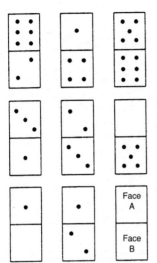

Face A		Face B	
0		0	
1		1	
2		2	
3		3	
4		4	
5		5	
6		6	

9.

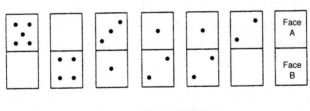

Face A		Face B	
0		0	
1		1	
2		2	
3		3	
4		4	
5		5	
6		6	

10.

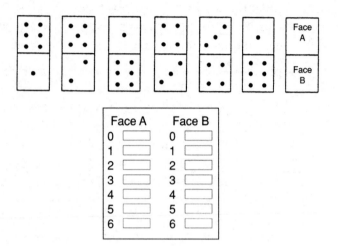

Data sufficiency

This test seeks to measure a candidate's ability to evaluate information and identify logical connections. You are provided with a passage describing a situation and a problem. You are also given a list of 5 additional pieces of information which may or may not resolve the problem. It is your task to identify the items which solve the problem. It is important that you do not waste time working out the answers but only the identity of the items of information required in order to establish the answer.

Practice exercises

1. A house plant and a decorative pot together retail at the inclusive price £3.75. Which two pieces of information do you require to establish the price of the pot before tax?

   A The pot cost twice as much as a non-decorative equivalent.

   B The pot costs three times as much as the plant, which is tax exempt.

   C VAT in the UK is currently 17.5 per cent.

   D An inclusive total is established by multiplying the exclusive price by the percentage rate of tax and adding this figure to the total.

   E The price of an item excluding tax can be worked out from the inclusive total by multiplying by 0.036 and subtracting the answer from the total.

   A. ☐   B. ☐   C. ☐   D. ☐   E. ☐

2. A group of friends charter a yacht for their annual holiday. Which three pieces of information are necessary to establish the amount that they each had to contribute towards the deposit?

   A Because it was the start of the season the trip cost £100; prices increased six-fold by July.

   B The boat could sleep a maximum of six but one berth was spare.

   C The holiday was to last two weeks.

   D A 10 per cent deposit was payable with the booking and is refundable on the safe return of the vessel.

   E Tony was going to come but cancelled when he realised the date would clash with his wife's birthday.

   A. ☐   B. ☐   C. ☐   D. ☐   E. ☐

3. John's 1990 salary was equal to three times his current salary. It was double what he earned in 1993. Which piece of information do you require in order to establish the percentage decrease he has had to endure since 1990?

    A Inflation over the period totalled 13 per cent.
    B John paid £5,250 tax in 1990.
    C The difference between John's salary in 1990 and 1993 totalled £7,000.
    D The rate of tax in 1990 was 25 per cent.
    E John's total current salary was only £1,750 greater than his 1990 tax bill.

    A. ☐   B. ☐   C. ☐   D. ☐   E. ☐

4. Peter lives on a small island a short distance off the mainland. His journey to work involves a boat trip and a train journey. Which two pieces of information do you require in order to establish the distance between Peter's house and the railway station?

    A The channel between the island and the mainland is 300 yards across.
    B It is exactly 100 metres from Peter's house to the pub.
    C The railway station is on the shore and Peter can see it from his front garden.
    D The locations of the house, pub and railway station form an equilateral triangle.
    E The only other building on Peter's island is a pub.

    A. ☐   B. ☐   C. ☐   D. ☐   E. ☐

5. Donna, Lucy and Chris between them own 80 marbles. Which two pieces of information allow you to establish how many of the marbles are Chris's?

   A Chris and Lucy have the same number.
   B Donna owns twice as many as Lucy.
   C Lucy used to have 25 until she gave some to her brother.
   D Fred, Lucy's brother, has three fewer than twice as many as Donna.

   A. ⬚   B. ⬚   C. ⬚   D. ⬚   E. ⬚

6. A piece of gold weighing 38 grams is not pure but mixed with base metals. Which three pieces of information do you need to establish the current market value of gold?

   A 80 per cent of the weight is due to the base metal.
   B The base metal is copper.
   C To convert from grams to ounces multiply by 0.03527.
   D The volume of the piece is 3 cubic centimetres.
   E Gold is worth £200 an ounce.

   A. ⬚   B. ⬚   C. ⬚   D. ⬚   E. ⬚

7. Steven, Kathy and Gino are all to drive from their home to Springville for an evening out. Gino in his Gti drives at 100 mph, Kathy in her 2CV more sensibly averages 35 mph while Steven never exceeds the speed limit of 60 mph. Which item of information do you require to establish the distance between their home town and Springville?

A Gino arrived in Springville 5 minutes before Steven and 10 minutes before Kathy.

B Despite all the stops at traffic lights, Kathy completed the journey in 35 minutes.

C Gino was booked for speeding.

D Steven completed the journey in 30 minutes.

A. ☐ B. ☐ C. ☐ D. ☐ E. ☐

8. The town hall can accommodate 40 rows of seats with between 25 and 37 seats per row. Which three items of information do you require to establish the percentage of the town's population which can be seated in the town hall when full?

A 20 rows can hold over 28 seats.

B The 1991 census of the population recorded the town as having a population of 22,350.

C The front 30 rows hold a total of 780 seats (an average of 26 per row).

D Since the closure of the shoe factory and the loss of 1,800 jobs people have moved away, leaving the population now 7% below the census total.

E In 1991, 18 per cent of the population were under five years of age.

F The overall average number of seats per row is 28.

A. ☐ B. ☐ C. ☐ D. ☐ E. ☐

9. Ford sell their basic 'Model T' at $4,250, or with extras for £5,050. Which item of information do you require to establish the most profitable option?

A   The price difference between options totals £800.
B   Ford aim at achieving a profit margin of 3 per cent.
C   The current basic model comes standard with items sold as extras 18 months ago.
D   The basic model achieves the 3 per cent profit margin.
E   Competition with Japanese car manufacturers means that Ford have to supply the extras to customers at cost price

A. ☐   B. ☐   C. ☐   D. ☐   E. ☐

10. In her will, Claire's instructions stated that all her possessions were to be sold and the cash shared out as follows: her second child was to receive £1,000 more than her third child, while her first born was to get three times as much as her second. Which three items of information are required to establish how much Martin was to receive?

A   Sue received £3,500.
B   Claire had four children.
C   Martin is 18 months older than Sue and one year younger than Peter.
D   Ken, Claire's youngest, was born two years after Sue.
E   The children mentioned in the will are called Sue, Peter and Martin.
F   Tragically, Claire outlived one of her children.

A. ☐   B. ☐   C. ☐   D. ☐   E. ☐

Logical reasoning

Each question makes a statement relating to a passage. It is your task to say whether the statement is necessarily true or false or if you cannot tell if it is true or false. You must base your decision only on the information contained in the passage, which you are expected to accept as completely true.

Passage 1

To activate the alarm in the computer department you enter the code 1234. The code 2345 provides cover for the print room as well as the computer department. Code 3456 activates the alarm for the whole building, while 4567 covers the sections for accounts and personnel. Staff are only to know the number for the whole building and the department in which they work. In addition to 3456, Scott and Betty have to remember 4567.

Questions

1. Scott and Betty work in the same department.

   True ⬚ False ⬚ Not possible to say ⬚

2. The maximum number of codes staff have to remember is two.

   True ⬚ False ⬚ Not possible to say ⬚

3. The code 2345 provides protection for the print room only.

   True ⬚ False ⬚ Not possible to say ⬚

Passage 2

Peter shared a father with Hilary but it is not Steven, the father of John, youngest son of Silvia (who is Hilary's mother).

Questions

4. Silvia had three children.

   True ☐   False ☐   Not possible to say ☐

5. Steven is the father of at least two of Silvia's children.

   True ☐   False ☐   Not possible to say ☐

6. Silvia is Peter's mother.

   True ☐   False ☐   Not possible to say ☐

7. John was the offspring of Steven and Silvia.

   True ☐   False ☐   Not possible to say ☐

Passage 3

All scientific statements that are valid state something which is shown by its proof to be so.

Questions

8. The passage demonstrates that all valid statements are scientific.

   True ☐   False ☐   Not possible to say ☐

9. A valid scientific statement must have proof.

   True ☐   False ☐   Not possible to say ☐

10. To be scientific, a statement must be valid.

    True [   ]   False [   ]   Not possible to say [   ]

11. A valid scientific statement must state something.

    True [   ]   False [   ]   Not possible to say [   ]

Passage 4

The result of subtracting the square of one number from the square of a second gives the same number as is obtained by adding the two numbers, subtracting the first from the second and then multiplying the results of these two calculations.

Questions

12. Whatever the values the same number is obtained.

    True [   ]   False [   ]   Not possible to say [   ]

13. The first number is the same as the second.

    True [   ]   False [   ]   Not possible to say [   ]

14. You could divide instead of multiply and get the same answer.

    True [   ]   False [   ]   Not possible to say [   ]

Passage 5

Nothing can arise out of nothing and matter cannot vanish but only be altered to take another form.

Questions

15. If you weigh something, burn it, then weigh it again the difference is the weight of the smoke.

    True ☐   False ☐   Not possible to say ☐

16. There is a finite amount of matter in the universe.

    True ☐   False ☐   Not possible to say ☐

17. It is impossible for the amount of diamonds in the universe to decrease.

    True ☐   False ☐   Not possible to say ☐

18. The amount of matter in the universe will neither increase nor decrease.

    True ☐   False ☐   Not possible to say ☐

19. It should be possible to achieve the alchemists' dream of turning base metals into gold.

    True ☐   False ☐   Not possible to say ☐

Answers to Chapter 5

Following procedures (page 133)

1.	B	6.	D
2.	E	7.	G, H
3.	E	8.	F
4.	D	9.	E, F, I
5.	E, G, H	10.	D

Speed and accuracy (page 137)

1.	3 pairs	9.	3 pairs	17.	3 pairs
2.	None	10.	2 pairs	18.	3 pairs
3.	2 pairs	11.	None	19.	2 pairs
4.	None	12.	2 pairs	20.	2 pairs
5.	2 pairs	13.	3 pairs	21.	1 pair
6.	None	14.	all 4	22.	1 pair
7.	2 pairs	15.	all 4	23.	1 pair
8.	2 pairs	16.	all four		

Composite test (page 143)

1.	A incorrect	B	correct
2.	A incorrect	B	incorrect
3.	A correct	B	incorrect
4.	A incorrect	B	correct
5.	A correct	B	correct
6.	A correct	B	correct
7	A incorrect	B	incorrect
8.	A correct	B	correct
9.	A correct	B	incorrect
10.	A correct	B	correct

Sentence sequence (page 149)

1.	1, 3, 4, 2	6.	2, 4, 1, 3	11.	2, 4, 1, 3
2.	1, 3, 4, 2	7.	2, 4, 3, 1	12.	3, 1, 4, 2
3.	1, 4, 3, 2	8.	3, 2, 1, 4	13.	3, 2, 4, 1
4.	3, 1, 2, 4	9.	4, 1, 3, 2	14.	3, 2, 4, 1
5.	2, 1, 3, 4	10.	3, 2, 1, 4		

Data interpretation (page 156)

1.	1	4.	3	7.	3	10.	4
2.	4	5.	1	8.	2	11.	1
3.	4	6.	4	9.	3	12.	1

Word link (page 161)

1.	golf club	7.	horse bench	13.	anarchy order
2.	ship hospital	8.	agree dispute	14.	red green
3.	manage regulate	9.	emperor empire	15.	Asia Europe
4.	top bottom	10.	horse hair	16.	competent defective
5.	king palace	11.	car petrol		
6.	construct retire	12.	light dark	17.	sketch appraises

Word swop (page 163)

1.	securing aimed	9.	sold made
2.	line press	10.	private consultants
3.	equal person	11.	worried pledged
4.	London association	12.	30,000 50,000
5.	grade range	13.	impressive predictable
6.	kicking back	14.	grandfather lord
7.	things naming	15.	ancient hard
8.	subject paragraph		

Dominoes (page 165)

1.	A:0	B:1		6.	A:4	B:1
2.	A:6	B:1		7.	A:1	B:6
3.	A:2	B:5		8.	A:2	B:4
4.	A:1	B:5		9.	A:6	B:3
5.	A:0	B:0		10.	A:2	B:5

Data sufficiency (page 170)

1.	B, C		6.	A, C, E
2.	A, B, D		7.	B
3.	C		8.	B, D, F
4.	B, D		9.	E
5.	A, B		10.	A, C, E

Logical reasoning (page 176)

1.	Not possible to say		11.	True
2.	False		12.	True
3.	False		13.	Not possible to say
4.	Not possible to say		14.	False
5.	Not possible to say		15.	Not possible to say
6.	Not possible to say		16.	Not possible to say
7.	True		17.	False
8.	False		18.	True
9.	True		19.	Not possible to say
10	False			

Chapter 6

Four mock tests to develop a winning test strategy

Mock test 1

Sentence sequencing, data interpretation and word link

This test comprises 28 questions. Allow yourself 15 minutes to attempt the test. Do not turn the page until you are ready to start.

Sentence sequencing questions

1. 1. Befuddled, she made her way to the door, not knowing who it could be at this hour.
    2. Suddenly, Collete was rudely awakened from her dream by an insistant knocking.
    3. She had won the national lottery and was about to receive the cheque for two million pounds from the television personality Joanna Lumley.
    4. Her heart nearly missed a beat when she saw the tall bespectacled man in the leather trenchcoat outside.

```
1 [ ]   1 [ ]   1 [ ]   1 [ ]
2 [ ]   2 [ ]   2 [ ]   2 [ ]
3 [ ]   3 [ ]   3 [ ]   3 [ ]
4 [ ]   4 [ ]   4 [ ]   4 [ ]
```

2. 1. This decline is mainly due to a collapse in the 20th century in the price of tin.
    2. Tin-mining has been a major industry in Cornwall for over 2,500 years.
    3. However, there is only one operating tin-mine left in Cornwall.
    4. In ancient times the Phoenicians traded tin with the Cornish.

```
1 [ ]   1 [ ]   1 [ ]   1 [ ]
2 [ ]   2 [ ]   2 [ ]   2 [ ]
3 [ ]   3 [ ]   3 [ ]   3 [ ]
4 [ ]   4 [ ]   4 [ ]   4 [ ]
```

3. 1. After all, the person behind you has been a learner too.
    2. Don't let the fact that you are the first in the queue influence your judgement about when to go.
    3. What you see when you look must decide your action and nothing else.
    4. As a learner you will be conscious of other drivers lining up behind you at junctions.

```
1 [ ]  1 [ ]  1 [ ]  1 [ ]
2 [ ]  2 [ ]  2 [ ]  2 [ ]
3 [ ]  3 [ ]  3 [ ]  3 [ ]
4 [ ]  4 [ ]  4 [ ]  4 [ ]
```

4. 1. This was the media response to the Preliminary Report on Homicide.
    2. The picture painted by the report itself is more complicated.
    3. 'The mentally ill commit one murder a fortnight' proclaimed the headlines.
    4. Home Office records suggest that 89 people with probable mental illness committed a murder between 1992 and 1993, more than one a fortnight and 12% of all murders.

```
1 [ ]  1 [ ]  1 [ ]  1 [ ]
2 [ ]  2 [ ]  2 [ ]  2 [ ]
3 [ ]  3 [ ]  3 [ ]  3 [ ]
4 [ ]  4 [ ]  4 [ ]  4 [ ]
```

5. 1. Input the relevant data, carry out a spell-check and print the document.
    2. Turn on the computer and monitor, key in your pass word and ensure you have entered the word-processing software.
    3. Name and save the file to an appropriate floppy disk and exit the program.
    4. Open a document file.

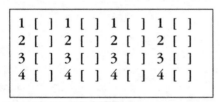

```
1 [ ]  1 [ ]  1 [ ]  1 [ ]
2 [ ]  2 [ ]  2 [ ]  2 [ ]
3 [ ]  3 [ ]  3 [ ]  3 [ ]
4 [ ]  4 [ ]  4 [ ]  4 [ ]
```

6. 1. A barrister will then be briefed to present the case in court before a judge.
    2. The solicitor may advise that there is a case and write to the opponent's solicitor.
    3. The potential litigant must first see a solicitor for preliminary advice.
    4. If liability is disputed and cannot otherwise be resolved, pleadings will be issued and a date set for a court hearing.

```
1 [ ]  1 [ ]  1 [ ]  1 [ ]
2 [ ]  2 [ ]  2 [ ]  2 [ ]
3 [ ]  3 [ ]  3 [ ]  3 [ ]
4 [ ]  4 [ ]  4 [ ]  4 [ ]
```

7. 1. In the re-examination, the witness has the opportunity
       to rectify any damage done in cross-examination.
    2. First, counsel examines his own witness-in-chief to
       ascertain facts.
    3. There are three stages to examining a witness in court.
    4. The witness is then made available to the opposition for
       cross-examination in which the witness's version of
       events is explored, clarified or demolished.

```
1 [ ]   1 [ ]   1 [ ]   1 [ ]
2 [ ]   2 [ ]   2 [ ]   2 [ ]
3 [ ]   3 [ ]   3 [ ]   3 [ ]
4 [ ]   4 [ ]   4 [ ]   4 [ ]
```

8. 1. Unlike many of his school friends who went to univer-
       sity, his family circumstances denied him any chance of
       higher education.
    2. However, he was soon back in Manchester on the staff
       of the *Evening Chronicle*, before transferring to the
       rival paper, the *Manchester Evening News*, in a move
       which was to shape his career.
    3. He therefore started to work on the *Blackpool Times* at
       the age of 17.
    4. Educated at Manchester Grammar School, Lord Ardwick
       reads the *Guardian* every day of his life.

```
1 [ ]   1 [ ]   1 [ ]   1 [ ]
2 [ ]   2 [ ]   2 [ ]   2 [ ]
3 [ ]   3 [ ]   3 [ ]   3 [ ]
4 [ ]   4 [ ]   4 [ ]   4 [ ]
```

9. 1. He was the prime mover behind the EuroTEC controversial refinancing package, and his resignation was not unexpected.
    2. Peter Heitman quit as Chief Executive as EuroTEC completed the final stage of its difficult restructuring plan.
    3. It caused the entertainment company's shares to rise 4 pence to 126p.
    4. The announcement stated that his replacement was Mr Montgomery, the ambitious and widely respected financial head of Paymore Bank, the principal lender to the troubled corporation.

```
1 [ ]   1 [ ]   1 [ ]   1 [ ]
2 [ ]   2 [ ]   2 [ ]   2 [ ]
3 [ ]   3 [ ]   3 [ ]   3 [ ]
4 [ ]   4 [ ]   4 [ ]   4 [ ]
```

10. 1. If you do, dial the number of the extension you want and you will automatically be connected.
    2. Alternatively, you must hang on to be dealt with by an operator.
    3. On certain telephone switchboards a recorded message will answer your call.
    4. It will ask you if you know the extension you want and whether or not you have a touch-tone phone.

```
1 [ ]   1 [ ]   1 [ ]   1 [ ]
2 [ ]   2 [ ]   2 [ ]   2 [ ]
3 [ ]   3 [ ]   3 [ ]   3 [ ]
4 [ ]   4 [ ]   4 [ ]   4 [ ]
```

Data interpretation questions

Country	Population (in millions)	Infant mortality per 1,000 births	Total number of births per 1,000	Agricultural area per person (in acres)
1980				
A	10	45	12	0.25
B	6	82	24	0.125
C	50	11	9	0.1
D	3	30	16	1.3
E	21	60	19	0.9
1990				
A	12	33	11	–
B	6.5	68	24	–
C	49	7	9	–
D	3.1	26	18	–
E	23	45	21	–

Key: – = Information not available.

11. Which country experienced the highest rate of infant mortality in 1990?

    1) E 2) A 3) B 4) C

1	2	3	4
[ ]	[ ]	[ ]	[ ]

12. Which countries have experienced an increase of two births per 1,000 over the decade?

    1) E D   2) A C   3) B C   4) D A

1	2	3	4
[ ]	[ ]	[ ]	[ ]

13. What is the percentage increase in population experienced by country E over the decade illustrated?

    1) 10.5 %   2) 8.5%   3) 9.0%   4) 9.5%

1	2	3	4
[ ]	[ ]	[ ]	[ ]

14. If in Country A the same amount of agricultural land is in use in 1990 as was the case in 1980, to what does the agricultural area per person decrease in 1990 (suggested answers are rounded down to two decimal places)?

    1) 0.20   2) 0.15   3) 0.30   4) none of these

1	2	3	4
[ ]	[ ]	[ ]	[ ]

Word link questions

15. NORTH   SOUTH
    Wales Scotland west   Sussex Kent east

16. CONGESTION   INFERENCE
    blockage superior   guess inferior conclusion
    infection

17. DYE   TAN
    cloth funeral shoe   coffin leather brown

18. METAL   COIN
    wood paper percussion   brass note news

19. SEASONABLE   RESPECTABLE
    untimely decreasing   upright pepper disgraceful
    winter

20. CENTIMETRE   INCH
    metre meter meat   foot claw gas

21. WEAK   GREEN
    month strong moon   experienced environmental
                             pliable

22. FUNCTION   DIGRESS
    work deviant immigrate   exodus toil deviate

23. BENEVOLENT   MALEVOLENT
    ridicule compliment   defiant hedonism dilapidated
    compliant

24. METAPHOR   SIMILE
    pious mystic undevout   irreverent devotee jinx

25. IGNORAMUS   ILLUMINATION
    obfuscation transfer   modest scarce encylcopaedist
    simple

26. DEFICIENT   MODERATE
    modification perfection gluttonous lapse stigma
    temperance

27. MALAPROPISM   LINGUISTICS
    solipsism behaviourism   mathematics psychology
    communism   engineering

28. AMORPHOUS   NEBULOUS
    abundance shower   torrent profusion enchantment
    harassment

End of Mock test 1

You will find the answers to this mock test at the end of the chapter.

Mock test 2

Data sufficiency

Allow yourself 20 minutes to attempt the 20 questions. Do not turn the page until you are ready to begin.

Data sufficiency

Situation 1

A factory is to commission two production lines. Production line 1 is to use the existing technology. Production line 2 is to use the latest innovations in technology and, while promising to achieve considerable advances in productivity, it will take longer to install and is likely to experience teething problems. Graph 1 illustrates the productive record of each production line. Refer to the graph in order to answer the following questions.

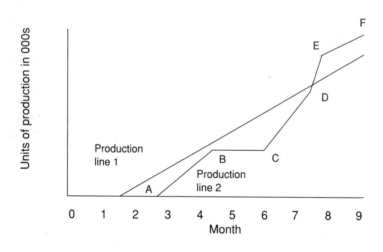

(Graph 1)

Question 1

In which month did production line 2 overtake production line 1 in the total number of units produced?

Answer

Question 2

From the information given, is it possible to attribute a reason why production line 1's record forms a straight line while production line 2's record takes the form of a polygon?

A = Yes, it is possible to attribute a reason
B = No, it is not possible to attribute a reason
C = You cannot tell if it is possible or not.

Answer

Question 3

The manager of production line 2 reported a complete break-down. At what point did this occur?

A Month 3
B During month 4
C Before month 4
D You cannot tell

Answer

Question 4

Consider the following questions (A and B) and indicate whether both, either or neither can be answered given the available data.

A   Can the duration of the reported breakdown be established?
B   Can the loss of production be quantified?

1. if both question A and B can be answered
2. if only question A can be answered
3. if only question B can be answered
4. if neither question can be answered

Answer

Situation 2

Fifty candidates sat a test and the number of candidates who scored more than a specific number of correct answers is illustrated in graph 2. Refer to this graph in order to answer the following questions.

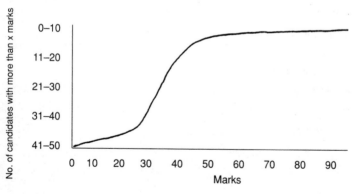

(Graph 2)

Question 5

What proportion of the candidates achieved over 50 correct marks?

A = The majority
B = A sizeable minority
C = Only a few
D = You cannot tell

Answer

Question 6

Is it possible to work out the median?

A = Yes, it is possible.
B = No, it is not possible.
C = You cannot tell if it is possible or not.

Answer

Question 7

A curve such as the one in graph 2 is called a:

A = Polygon
B = Ogive
C = Parallel
D = None of these

Answer

Question 8

Consider the following questions (A and B) and indicate whether both, either or neither can be answered given the available data.

A   Did the 50 candidates do well or badly in the test?

B   How many candidates got more than 70 marks out of 100?

1.   if both questions A and B can be answered
2.   if only question A can be answered
3.   if only question B can be answered
4.   if neither question can be answered

Answer

Situation 3

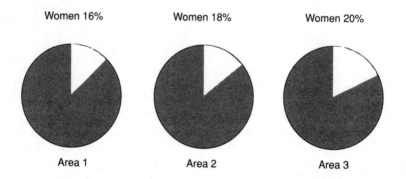

Women 16%   Women 18%   Women 20%

Area 1   Area 2   Area 3

The three pie charts demonstrate the level of unemployment among women as a percentage of the economically active population in three areas. The economically active population excludes people too old or too young to work. The total economically active population for the three areas is 55,000.

Question 9

Is it possible to work out the percentage level of unemployment for the total populations of all three areas?

A = Yes, it is possible.
B = No, it is not possible.
C = You cannot tell if it is possible or not.

Answer

Question 10

What is the mean percentage rate of unemployment for economically active women across the three areas (assuming that the areas have equal populations)?

A = 18%
B = 54%
C = 3%
D = You cannot tell

Answer

Question 11

How many unemployed women are there?

A = 22,500
B = More than half the total
C = Less than half the total
D = You cannot tell

Answer

Question 12

Consider the following questions (A and B) and indicate whether both, either or neither can be answered given the available data.

A   Why are there more unemployed men than women?
B   What is the total working population across the three areas?

1.   if both questions A and B can be answered
2.   if only question A can be answered
3.   if only question B can be answered
4.   if neither question can be answered

Answer

Situation 4

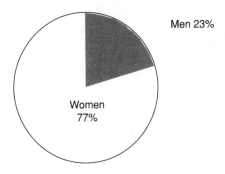

The gender of customers who requested childcare
facilities at the shopping arcade

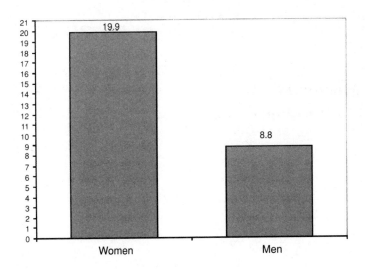

The percentage of customers wanting childcare facilities
who were willing to pay for the service

The managers of a shopping arcade undertook a process of customer consultation and found that high on the list of facilities requested by customers was a shoppers' crèche. In total 800 customers took part in the survey which was conducted during working hours between Monday 14 and Wednesday 16 May.

Question 13

What percentage of women who requested childcare facilities were also willing to pay to use the service?

A = 19.9%
B = 23%
C = 77%
D = You cannot tell

Answer

Question 14

What percentage of male customers requested childcare facilities?

A = 77%
B = 8.8%
C = 2.3%
D = You cannot tell

Answer

Question 15

Is it true to say that 100 per cent of customers who took part in the survey wanted childcare facilities at the arcade?

A   =   Yes
B   =   No
C   =   You cannot tell

Answer

Question 16

Consider the following questions (A and B) and indicate whether both, either or neither can be answered given the available data.

A   What is the ratio between men and women customers who wanted childcare facilities?

B   How might the result have been affected had the management arranged for the survey to be carried out over the weekend rather than during the working week?

    1   if both questions A and B can be answered
    2   if only question A can be answered
    3   if only question B can be answered
    4. if neither question can be answered

Answer

Situation 5

The programmes director of a local radio station received the cohort below, which compares the age and gender of listeners. During the period to which the cohort refers, 52 per cent of the station's audience were women. Most mornings 125,000 families tune in for the breakfast show.

Use this information and the data contained in the cohort to answer the questions which follow.

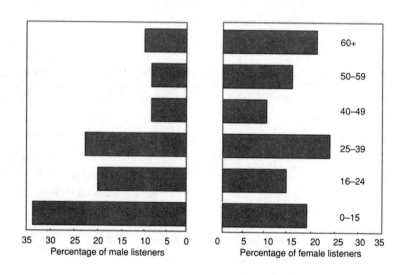

Age/gender cohort of local radio station listeners

Question 17

What percentage of male listeners are aged 15 years or under?

A = 0–15%
B = Between 15 and 20%
C = Between 30 and 35%
D = You cannot tell

Answer

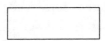

Question 18

What percentage of women aged between 16 and 24 years tune into the station?

A = Just under 15%
B = 20%
C = 100%
D = You cannot tell

Answer

Question 19

What percentage of women listeners are aged 45 years?

A = Just over 10%
B = Just under 10%
C = You cannot tell

Answer

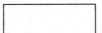

Question 20

Consider the following questions and indicate whether both, either or neither can be answered given the available data.

A   What percentage of listeners are aged between 25 and 39 years?

B   With which age group is the station most popular?

1.   if both questions A and B can be answered
2.   if only question A can be answered
3.   if only question B can be answered
4.   if neither question can be answered

Answer

End of Mock test 2

You will find the answers to this mock test at the end of the chapter.

Mock test 3

Reading comprehension

Over the page you will find 15 questions relating to three passages. Allow yourself 20 minutes to complete the test. Do not turn the page until you are ready to begin.

Reading comprehension

Passage 1

He that is nourished by the acorns that he picked up under an oak, or the apples he gathered from the trees in the wood, has certainly appropriated them to himself. Nobody can deny but the nourishment is his. I ask, then, when did they begin to be his? when he digested? or when he ate? or when he boiled? or when he brought them home? or when he picked them up? And it is plain, if the first gathering made them not his, nothing else could. That labour put a distinction between them and common. That added something to them more than Nature, the common mother of all, and so they became his private right...

His labour hath taken it out of the hands of Nature where it was common, and belonged equally to all her children, and hath thereby appropriated it to himself...

It will, perhaps, be objected to this, that if gathering the acorns or other fruits of the earth, etc, makes a right to them, then anybody may engross as much as he will. To which I answer, Not so. The same law of Nature that does by this means give us property, does also bound that property too. 'God had given us all things richly.' Is the voice of reason confirmed by inspiration? But how far has He given it us – 'to enjoy'? As much as anyone can make use of to advantage of life before it spoils, so much he may by his labour fix a property in. Whatever is beyond this is more than his share, and belongs to others...

He who gathered as much of the wild fruit, killed, caught, or tamed as many of the beasts as he could – he that so employed his pains about any of the spontaneous products of Nature as any way to alter them from the state Nature put them in, by placing any of his labour on them, did thereby acquire a property in them, but if they perished in his possession without their due use – if the fruits rotted or the venison putrefied before he could spend it, he offended against the common law of Nature, and was liable to be punished: he invaded his neighbour's share, for he had no right farther than his use called for any of them, and they might serve to afford him conveniences of life.

John Locke, Section V, *An Essay Concerning the True Original, Extent and End of Civil Government* (1690)

Question 1

The primary purpose of this passage is to:

A   Describe the way in which we lived before civilisation

B   Promote the equal sharing of the world's scarce resources

C   Investigate the basis for legitimate private property

D   None of these

Answer

Question 2

The objection that Locke's argument allows one to 'engross as much as he will' fails because:

A   God has given us all things richly so we can take as much as we like

B   The fruit will rot and the venison will putrefy so there is no point taking more than you need

C   The law of Nature dictates that if we take more than we can use we have taken something which belongs to others

D   None of these

Answer

Question 3

Which of the following words describe the tone of the passage?

A   Humorous?
B   Contrived?
C   Journalistic?
D   None of these?

Answer

Question 4

Locke suggests that it is unequivocal that we have appropriated something for ourselves if we:

A   Collected it and carried it away
B   Have eaten and digested it
C   Stored it for winter
D   None of these

Answer

Question 5

In the passage Locke argues that you can acquire something as your own property if you:

A   Share it with others
B   Inherit it
C   Seize a neighbour's share
D.   None of these

Answer

Passage 2

The produce of labour constitutes the natural recompense or wages of labour.

In that original state of things, which precedes both the appropriation of land and the accumulation of stock, the whole produce of labour belongs to the labourer. He has neither landlord nor master to share with him.

Had this state continued, the wages of labour would have augmented with all those improvements in its productive powers, to which the division of labour gives occasion. All things would gradually have become cheaper. They would have been produced by a smaller quantity of labour; and as the commodities produced by equal quantities of labour would naturally in this state of things be exchanged for one another, they would have been purchased likewise with the produce of a small quantity.

But though all things would have become cheaper in reality, in appearance many things might have become dearer than before, or have been exchanged for a greater quantity of other goods. Let us suppose, for example, that in the greater part of employments the productive powers of labour had been improved tenfold, or that a day's labour could produce only ten times the quantity of work which it had done originally, but that in a particular employment they had been improved only to double, or that a day's labour could produce only twice the quantity of work which it had done before. In exchanging the produce of a day's labour in the greater part of employments, for that of a day's labour in this particular one, ten times the original quantity of work in them would purchase only twice the original quantity in it. Any particular quantity in it, therefore, a pound weight, for example, would appear to be five times dearer than before. In reality, however, it would be twice as cheap. Though it required five times the quantity of other goods to purchase it, it would require only half the quantity of labour either to purchase or to produce it. The acquisition, therefore, would be twice as easy as before.

Adam Smith, Of the Wages of Labour, Chapter VIII, Volume 1, *The Wealth of Nations* (1776)

Question 6

The passage addresses which of the following issues?

A   The effect of division of labour on productive power
B   The effect on prices if labourers were to keep all the product of their labour
C   The effect on prices if labourers kept all the product of their labour and their labour benefited from improvements in productive power.
D   None of these

Answer

Question 7

If labourers were to keep all the product of their labour, Smith states things would become cheaper in:

A   Reality
B   Appearance
C   The market-place
D   None of these

Answer

Question 8

If the productive power of labour is improved tenfold, Smith claimed:

A   Things would appear five times cheaper
B   Things would in reality be twice as cheap
C   Things would appear five times dearer
D   None of these

Answer

Question 9

Smith holds that commodities would continue to be exchanged in equal quantities only if:

A   One product benefited more from improvements in productive power than the other
B   Labour was divided, land appropriated and stock accumulated
C   Both products benefited equally from improvements in productive power
D   None of these

Answer

Question 10

According to Smith, while in reality things would become cheaper, in appearance:

A   All things would become dearer
B   Some things would become dearer
C   Some things might become dearer
D   None of these

Answer

```
┌──────────────┐
│              │
└──────────────┘
```

Passage 3

Now suppose that the average amount of the daily necessaries of a labouring man require six hours of average labour for their production. Suppose, moreover, six hours of average labour to be also realised in a quantity of gold equal to three shillings. Then three shillings would be the Price, or the monetary expression of the Daily Value of that man's Labouring Power. If he worked daily six hours he would daily produce a value sufficient to buy the average amount of his daily necessaries, or to maintain himself as a labouring man.

But our man is a wages labourer. He must, therefore, sell his labouring power to a capitalist. If he sells it at three shillings daily, or 18 shillings weekly, he sells it at its value. Suppose him to be a spinner. If he works six hours daily he will add to the cotton a value of three shillings daily. This value, daily added by him, would be the exact equivalent for the wages, or the price of his labouring power, received daily. But in that case no surplus value or surplus produce whatever would go to the capitalist. Here, then, we come to the rub…

The value of the labouring power is determined by the

quantity of labour necessary to maintain or reproduce it, but the use of that labouring power is only limited by the active energies and the physical strength of the labourer... Take the example of our spinner. We have seen that, to daily reproduce his labouring power, he must daily reproduce a value of three shillings, which he will do by working six hours daily. But this does not disable him from working ten or twelve or more hours a day. But by paying the daily or weekly value of the spinner's labouring power, the capitalist has acquired the right of using the labouring power during the whole day or week. He will, therefore, make him work, say, daily for twelve hours. Over and above the six hours required to replace his wages, or the value of his labouring power, he will, therefore, have to work six other hours, which I shall call surplus labour, which surplus labour will realise itself in a surplus value and a surplus produce. If our spinner, for example, by his daily labour of six hours, added three shillings' value to the cotton, a value forming an exact equivalent to his wages, he will, in twelve hours, add six shillings' worth to the cotton, and produce a proportional surplus of yarn. As he has sold his labouring power to the capitalist, the whole value or produce created by him belongs to the capitalist, the owner... of his labouring power.

Karl Marx, Production of Surplus Value, Section VIII, *Wages, Price and Profit* (1865)

Question 13

Identify from the following a correct restatement of the main idea of the passage:

A The amount of surplus value depends on the ratio in which the working day is prolonged over the time it takes for the working man to replace his wages

B A general rise in the rate of wages would result in a fall in the general rate of profit

C It is the constant tendency of capitalists to stretch the working day to its utmost physically possible length

D None of these

Answer

Question 14

Which of the following statements best describes the approach taken by Marx in the passage?

A He refutes a stated view

B He sets out be expansive

C His objective is to compare and contrast

D None of these

Answer

Question 15

According to Marx the spinner's daily necessities require:

A   Three shillings
B   Six hours of average labour
C   A 12-hour working day
D   None of these

Answer

End of Mock test 3

You will find the answers to this mock test at the end of the chapter.

Mock test 4

Logical reasoning

Over the page you will find a mock test comprising 36 questions. Complete the test in 25 minutes.

Do not turn the page until you are ready to begin.

Logical reasoning

Passage 1

Research suggests that a sustained increase in spending on infrastructure is associated with an increase in macro economic growth, albeit not as convincingly in the data as intuition would suggest.

Question 1

High levels of investment spent on infrastructure are fairly well correlated with economic growth.

A   True
B   False
C   You cannot tell

Answer

Question 2

High spending tends to promote productivity gains and faster economic growth.

A   True
B   False
C   You cannot tell

Answer

Question 3

Building a new rail link might be beneficial to macro growth

A   True
B   False
C   You cannot tell

Answer

Passage 2

Quarter 3, 1999 data showed that the US economy expanded by just 0.4% against a 1.1% rise in the first quarter of 1999.

All that year, forecasters argued that the US dollar was over-valued, yet it continued to appreciate against every other currency. Finally, in the third quarter the dollar weakened.

Question 4

The US economic growth cooled markedly during 1999.

A   True
B   False
C   You cannot tell

Answer

Question 5

Depreciation of the US currency could easily gather momentum during the remainder of 1999.

A   True
B   False
C   You cannot tell

Answer

Question 6

Economic growth was a factor behind the appreciation of the US dollar.

A   True
B   False
C   You cannot tell

Answer

Question 7

An American coming to Europe in the fall of 1999 found he could buy more with his dollars than when he visited Europe earlier that year.

A   True
B   False
C   Cannot tell

Answer

Passage 3

In a survey, companies' total cashflow position was found to have worsened slightly; 22% reported cashflow problems compared with 19% in the previous survey. However, this result is still well below the trend average of 29% over the life of the survey.

Question 8

This still is a pretty impressive result.

A   True
B   False
C   You cannot tell

Answer

Question 9

The survey suggests that the respondents' cashflow management has improved over the life of the survey.

A   True
B   False
C   You cannot tell

Answer

Question 10

Late payment remains the main source of cashflow problems for respondents.

A   True
B   False
C   You cannot tell

Answer

Passage 4

Data show that two-thirds of companies surveyed advertised on the Internet compared with just half of companies surveyed 18 months ago.

Question 11

The number of companies advertising on the Internet has increased markedly.

A   True
B   False
C   You cannot tell

Answer

Question 12

In terms of its impact on company performance and possibly also in terms of its implications for the wider economy, the survey suggests that Internet use has not yet reached it full potential.

A   True

B   False

C   Cannot tell

Answer

Passage 5

Sixteen per cent of firms report using the Internet in central purchasing, of which almost 43% report making slight cost savings, 5% report making significant savings, 28% suggest that it is too early to tell whether or not savings are being made, while the remaining respondents said that no savings were being made.

Question 13

It is fair to conclude that for some respondents use of the Internet has resulted in a reduction in the cost of central purchases.

A   True

B   False

C   You cannot tell

Answer

Question 14

The majority of respondents who used the Internet for central purchasing either saw no cost benefit or reported that it was too early to tell.

A   True
B   False
C   You cannot tell

Answer

Question 15

The majority of respondents used the Internet for central purchases.

A   True
B   False
C   You cannot tell

Answer

Passage 6

Sales performance varies by industrial sector in terms of sales and orders, retailing performed least well and business and other services performed best. Industries with above sector-average sales include construction, wholesale, and hotel and catering. While manufacturing sales remain below the industrial sector-average, sales have improved for this and the last three years.

Question 16

Business and other services outperform other sectors in sales and orders.

A   True
B   False
C   You cannot tell

Answer

Question 17

Manufacturing continues to pick up.

A   True
B   False
C   You cannot tell

Answer

Question 18

Considerable price pressures exist in retailing.

A   True
B   False
C   You cannot tell

Answer

Question 19

Transport and communication and hotel and catering were the only sectors reporting above sector-average sales.

A   True

B   False

C   You cannot tell

Answer

Question 20

The sector Business and Other Services included wholesale.

A   True

B   False

C   Cannot tell

Answer

Passage 7

Net export balance sharply rose to 16% following net balances of 4% each in the previous two surveys; 41% of companies reported higher export orders against 25% reporting lower export orders, compared with levels of 33% and 29% six months ago.

Question 21

More companies report lower export orders than six months ago.

A   True
B   False
C   You cannot tell

Answer

Question 22

All companies are expanding sales of goods and services abroad.

A   True
B   False
C   You cannot tell

Answer

Question 23

More companies have reported higher export orders.

A   True
B   False
C   Cannot tell

Answer

Question 24

Export orders show surprise growth.

A   True
B   False
C   You cannot tell

Answer

Passage 8

Companies surveyed reported a negative net price balance of 3% in the second half of 2000. Nineteen per cent of firms reported raising prices while 22% reported cutting prices. This result extends the period of price cuts to three years.

Question 25

All companies are lowering the prices that they charge their customers.

A   True
B   False
C   You cannot tell

Answer

Question 26

Falling prices are squeezing profits.

A   True
B   False
C   You cannot tell

Answer

Question 27

The period of price cutting has continued into the second half of 2000.

A   True
B   False
C   You cannot tell

Answer

Question 28

It is no coincidence that the percentage difference between firms that report raising prices and those cutting prices is the same as the second half percentage figure for negative net price balance.

A   True
B   False
C   You cannot tell

Answer

The diagram illustrates what action an employer must take following new government legislation on employee pensions.

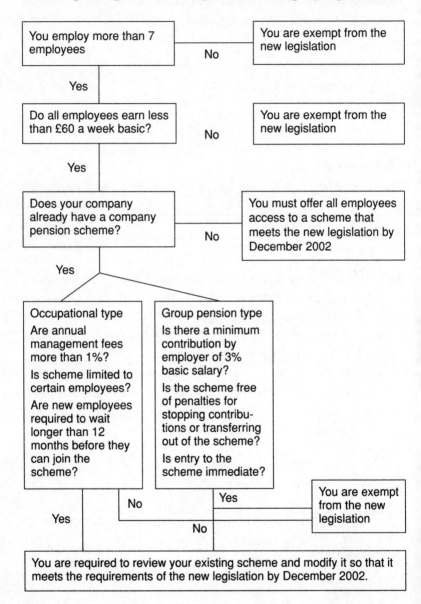

Questions

29. You employ 6 employees and currently offer an occupational type scheme which has a management fee each year of 1%.

No action required	Action required	Not enough information provided to decide

30. Your current occupational scheme is not offered to full-time employees.

No action required	Action required	Not enough information provided to decide

31. Your company has a group pension scheme. Directors of the company receive a contribution of 10% of basic salary after 3 months' service. All staff receive a minimum employer contribution of 3%. The scheme is free of penalties and all staff may join immediately.

No action required	Action required	Not enough information provided to decide

32. Nine out of 13 of your employees earn less than the legislationally exempt minimum salary.

No action required	Action required	Not enough information provided to decide

33. Entry to your occupational scheme is offered to all employees, there is no annual management fee and employees wait 10 months to join.

No action required	Action required	Not enough information provided to decide

34 Your company already has a pension scheme which allows new employees to join immediately and has no penalties for stopping or starting.

No action required	Action required	Not enough information provided to decide

35. You offer a group pension scheme for all employees after 3 months' service with no exit penalties.

No action required	Action required	Not enough information provided to decide

36. A member of staff declines to join your company complaint scheme.

No action required	Action required	Not enough information provided to decide

End of Mock test 4

You will find the answers to this mock test at the end of the chapter.

Answers to Chapter 6

Mock test 1

1.	3, 2, 1, 4	15.	west east
2.	2, 4, 3, 1	16.	blockage conclusion
3.	4, 2, 3, 1	17.	cloth leather
4.	3, 1, 2, 4	18.	paper note
5.	2, 4, 1, 3	19.	untimely disgraceful
6.	3, 2, 4, 1	20.	metre foot
7.	3, 2, 4, 1	21.	strong experienced
8.	4, 1, 3, 2	22.	work deviate
9.	2, 1, 4, 3	23.	compliant defiant
10.	3, 4, 1, 2	24.	mystic devotee
11.	3	25.	obfuscation encyclopaedist
12.	1	26.	perfection gluttonous
13.	4	27.	behaviourism psychology
14.	1	28.	abundance profusion

Mock test 2

1.	7	11.	D
2.	A	12.	3
3.	B	13.	A
4.	1	14.	C
5.	C	15.	B
6.	A	16.	2
7.	B	17.	C
8.	3	18.	A
9.	B	19.	C
10.	A	20.	1

Mock test 3

Passage 1	Passage 2	Passage 3
1. C	6. C	11. C
2. C	7. A	12. B
3. B	8. D	13. A
4. B	9. C	14. B
5. D	10. C	15. B

Mock test 4

1. True	21. False
2. Cannot tell	22. False
3. True	23. True
4. True	24. Cannot tell
5. Cannot tell	25. False (19% raised prices)
6. Cannot tell	26. Cannot tell
7. False	27. True
8. True	28. False (the figures are unconnected so it must be a coincidence)
9. Cannot tell	29. Not enough information
10. Cannot tell	30. Action required
11. True	31. No action required
12. Cannot tell	32. Action required
13. True	33. No action required
14. True	34. Not enough information provided
15. False (only 16% did)	35. Not enough information provided
16. True	36. No action required
17. True	
18. Cannot tell	
19. False	
20. False	